A
STRATEGY
FOR
PEACE

A
STRATEGY
FOR
PEACE

**HUMAN VALUES
AND THE THREAT OF WAR**

SISSELA
BOK

PANTHEON BOOKS · NEW YORK

Library of Congress Cataloging-in-Publication Data

Bok, Sissela.
  A strategy for peace: human values and the threat of
war
  Includes index.
  1. Peace. 2. Nuclear arms control. I. Title.
JX1952.B558   1989   327.1′72   88-25524
ISBN 0-394-55670-4

Book Design by Marie-Hélène Fredericks

Manufactured in the United States of America

First Edition

CONTENTS

ACKNOWLEDGMENTS

This book constitutes an expanded version of the two
Joan and Erik Erikson Lectures that I delivered in
October 1985 at Harvard University. It was an honor and
a great pleasure for me to be associated with Joan and Erik
Erikson in this undertaking. I can remember the first time
I read Erik Erikson's *Childhood and Society,* over thirty
years ago, and in particular his illuminating discussion of
the stages of the human life cycle. I have followed the
working out and enrichment of his thought in his subsequent writings; and admired, as well, the work of Joan
Erikson, with her artful weaving of symbols—including
those for the stages of the life cycle—into textiles, and of
works of art into the texture of discussions about ideas
and human beings.

I wish to thank all who discussed the lectures and the
book manuscript with me, and in particular Daniel Calla-
han, Robert Coles, Randall Forsberg, Carol Gilligan,
Samuel Gorovitz, Russell Hardin, Stanley Hoffmann,
Martha Nussbaum, Joseph Nye, Susan Okin, Amélie
Rorty, John Shattuck, Judith Shklar, Claire Simon, Andreas Teuber, Dennis Thompson, Lloyd Weinreb, and
David Wong. My warm thanks go to Susan Rabiner and
all at Pantheon Books who helped with the manuscript.

As with my previous writings, Derek Bok, Hilary Bok, and other members of my family offered encouragement, indispensable criticism, and an ongoing conversation over the years about the issues I take up in this book. Finally, I owe a special debt of gratitude to my mother, Alva Myrdal. She conveyed, during her last years, increasing impatience with the abstract talk of peace and the symbolic gestures in its name that too often take the place of serious cooperation to reduce the threat of war. And she discussed with me different ways to encourage more practical and comprehensive approaches to reducing that threat —beginning with efforts to combat the many practices of violence and corruption in personal, societal, and international life that help stifle cooperation. My book had its origin in our talks during that period, beginning in the early 1980s. I dedicate it, as she would have wished, not to her but to her grandchildren and great-grandchildren.

INTRODUCTION

The purpose of this book is to propose steps toward a secure and lasting peace that are practical, nonutopian, and in keeping with widely shared human values. The peoples of the world have never known such a peace; many doubt they ever will. Yet it has now become the only safe alternative to collective self-destruction.

Erik Erikson has suggested an analogy between the "species-wide nuclear crisis" that humanity now confronts and the crises that individuals face in the course of illnesses or great challenges.[1] These personal crises arise each time children acquire a new perspective on themselves and on the world—in learning to sit, for instance, or to fight or run about. Throughout life, each new crisis makes individuals vulnerable even as it gives them an opportunity for further growth through their very effort at mastery.

Using Erikson's analogy, we may ask: Does our present predicament offer similar scope for mastery and growth? Can it challenge peoples and governments to gain control over new capabilities that risk the annihilation of all? Can it, in this process, free nations to harness their formidable resources to cope more adequately with hunger and illness, poverty and environmental deterioration?

I am convinced that the present crisis offers scope for such changes. Proposals abound for how to bring them about. During the last few years, governments have expressed renewed determination to break the momentum of the arms race and to redirect attention and resources to the most urgent global problems. Yet time presses. We cannot afford merely to wait for states to achieve a lasting settlement on their own, much less expect a world government to be instituted and made to work adequately in time to forestall disaster. And it is irresponsible to entrust the survival of humanity to the vagaries of a world balance of power or to naive faith in the unerring judgment of the growing number of persons with the power to trigger a nuclear war. We have no choice but to consider most urgently how best to take concerted and meaningful action at every level—international, national, local and, as I shall argue, even personal—in response to the crisis in which we find ourselves.

Such collective action will remain inadequate, I suggest in this book, without renewed attention to the fundamental human values that have traditionally promoted the cohesion and survival of communities under stress. Nations will never attain even the minimal level of trust needed for cooperation on the unprecedented scale that has now become imperative without taking their bearings from such fundamental values. In the pages to come, I shall set forth a framework of four principles of conduct, basic to a great many moral, religious, and political traditions. When these principles are violated, utter distrust is the most reasonable response, among individuals as among governments and peoples, even though it also hampers collective responses to danger.

The steps that I propose address not only the overarching nuclear threat to human survival but also the many non-nuclear wars that plague our century. These

wars have taken over seventeen million lives, most of
them civilian, since the end of the Second World War and
have sent countless millions from their homes. By the next
century, several nations now bitterly enmeshed in regional
conflicts will in all likelihood be nuclear powers. Even if
the threat of nuclear war were to be ended, it is far from
clear that the world would be more peaceful in the absence
of fundamental changes. Indeed, as the historian Michael
Howard and others have pointed out, a world without the
sobering fear of nuclear war might be even more conflict-
ridden and brutal so long as the present pattern of world
politics remains largely unchanged.[2]

Though deterrence may well have forced unaccus-
tomed prudence on nations holding the power of total
destruction, nothing guarantees that it can do so indefi-
nitely. And the early hopes for immediate and total nuclear disarmament have likewise been tempered by the
realization that nuclear weapons cannot be disinvented.
Meanwhile, more gradual and limited approaches to arms
control still leave great risks for mankind. Progress has
been agonizingly slow toward even such modest agreements as we now have, and these are subject to continuing
threats of reversal. Even if the superpowers could achieve
their most ambitious hopes for arms control agreements,
the remaining weapons would suffice for destroying the
world many times over.

The dilemma remains. On the one hand, the nuclear
threat to humanity is intolerable; on the other hand, the
reasons for mutual fear and distrust are real enough and
powerful enough to keep nations from reducing the threat
decisively, let alone wiping it out entirely. Understandably, the threat has so far occupied center stage. Our hope,
I suggest, lies in taking distrust equally seriously.

Ten years ago, in *Lying: Moral Choice in Public and
Private Life,* I wrote of trust as a social good to be pro-

tected just as much as the air we breathe or the water we drink.[3] In the present book, I pursue this analogy by speaking of a social environment that is as much at risk as our natural environment. We witness the cumulative damage from countless disparate activities to the earth's oceans and waterways, its atmosphere, even its ozone layer; the consensus is growing that nations must combat this damage together in order to succeed and that merely allowing present policies to continue invites ecological disaster. It is every bit as urgent, I shall argue, to reduce the damage to the social atmosphere in which all human interaction takes place and to preserve the minimum of trust that is its prime constituent.

To be sure, a measure of caution and distrust is indispensable. Pure trust is no more conducive to survival in the social environment than is pure oxygen in the earth's atmosphere. But too high a level of distrust stifles efforts at cooperation as much as severe pollution impairs health. Just as the earth's atmosphere requires a proportion of oxygen neither so low as to cause living organisms to die nor so high as to produce uncontrollable fires, so human societies can thrive only within a certain range of combined trust and cautious distrust. Too much trust invites exploitation and abuse and is itself life-threatening; yet if distrust becomes too overpowering, societies can no longer function, any more than families or communities, much less plan for long-term survival.

Up to now, the debate over how to defuse the danger to mankind has focused, on all sides of the political spectrum, on issues of military security and on the pros and cons of arms reduction. Whether or not to develop different weapons systems; whether to freeze or speed up research, testing, and deployment of different systems; by what procedures to try to prevent an accidental or irrational nuclear attack; whether to aim nuclear missiles at population centers or at military targets; whether it is possible to have defenses against a nuclear assault that do not at the same time serve offensive purposes—these issues have dominated the debate. And surely they are of crucial importance.[4] But given the existing level of distrust, it is no wonder that negotiations have moved at a snail's pace and at times collapsed altogether. Even if a breakthrough should occur, it could be quickly halted in times of stress as long as strong reasons remain for the underlying distrust.

Taking distrust seriously calls for governments to continue to exercise all necessary caution and distrust while moving more forcefully to avoid either succumbing to, or inspiring, needless and debilitating distrust. It calls for more imaginative efforts to restore confidence and for a reevaluation of all practices that breed distrust. Among the latter it will be necessary to reexamine, in such a light, not only different military policies but also the many forms of economic and psychological warfare, the world-spanning smog of disinformation, the surreptitious and overt moves to cheat on international treaties, human rights violations, the support of regional wars, and the encouragement of terrorism.

Such a reevaluation of national policies is long overdue. Governments can no longer afford to violate fundamental moral standards at will in their conduct of foreign relations. However often these standards have been ignored or rejected in international relations in the past, and however reasonable the skepticism at hearing them hypocritically intoned by leaders bent on conquest and exploitation, they have now become indispensable for sheer self-protection.

In proposing a framework of moral principles to serve a strategy for peace, this book rejects the many calls for a "new ethics" or for some worldwide religious or psychological or political conversion after which peace will arrive, as it were, by itself.[5] We cannot count on such a transformation of society to wipe out the threat of war. Conversions, moreover, can go astray and new ideologies disappoint. When mass transformations bypass reflection, they open the way to uncritical acceptance of beliefs; they can then find unanticipated and brutal outlets, as we have surely witnessed in our own century.[6] The verdict attributed to Voltaire still holds: "Those who can make you believe absurdities can make you commit atrocities."

Yet the calls for a new approach speak to a genuine need. I suggest that we think of it as a need not for new values but, rather, for a more purposeful effort to adhere to existing ones; not for a new morality or system of ethics but, rather, for challenging the depth and scope of our present moral traditions; and thus not for some utopian scheme of universal harmony but, rather, for singling out the perspective, the guiding principles, and the practical strategy most suited to coping with the present crisis.[7]

I draw on long-standing traditions of moral, religious, and political reflection and on the examples of certain remarkable human lives for such a perspective and such a set of principles. With respect to the concepts of peace and of strategy, I rely on perhaps the most forceful and articulate investigations of each: Immanuel Kant's essay "Perpetual Peace" and *On War* by Carl von Clausewitz.[8] Their views are often thought antithetical. I hope to show, on the contrary, how the thinking of each can enrich that of the other and why the time is ripe for putting both inquiries to new use. It is now possible to examine their insights in the light of our century's experience, not only with unprecedented threats to collective survival but also with innovative countervailing forces of increasing strength—political, diplomatic, institutional, scholarly, and cultural—in such a way as to generate a strategy more capable of meeting the present threat.

In the last half of the book, I turn to the practical uses to which a strategy for peace can be put, both in cutting back on policies that increase distrust and thus the threat of war, and in promoting collective security. Such a strategy suggests new opportunities for states, large and small, to begin reversing the cumulative damage to the environment in which their interactions take place, much as they are moving to counteract the deterioration of the earth's atmosphere and waters. It suggests opportunities, as well, for action by public officials, international agencies, religious bodies, the news media, and multinational corporations. And for private citizens, the strategy sets forth ways to respond to the shared crisis through efforts in personal and community life as well as through organized measures to affect government policy at home and abroad.

The perspective, the set of principles, and the practical measures that the strategy calls for are needed as much, moreover, in efforts to change the atmosphere within nations as among them. Oppression, civil war, or a combination of the two still burden most of the world's peoples. Even in countries better off than most in those regards, factionalism and distrust stand in the way of coping forcefully with urgent problems. When public officials disregard fundamental values in the conduct of foreign policy, they are led to do so domestically as well, if for no other reason than to conceal their activities and to silence critics. Such conduct corrupts public life, undermines the accountability without which further abuses thrive, and adds to the already strong public distrust of politics and government. It should come as no surprise that many in private life lower their standards accordingly, nor that so many young people should refuse to vote or to take any part in public life. No nation can long afford to allow what its leaders claim are the exigencies of foreign policy to undermine domestic life so severely.

My suggestions are not meant to be exhaustive. In calling attention to ways of changing the context in which issues of war and peace are now debated, I hope, rather, to invite further suggestions, further debate. The climate of distrust, along with all the policies that contribute to it, now becloud that context. There are opportunities for everyone to help bring about a reversal—for in the end, it is human beings, singly and collectively, who help *create* the context.

A
STRATEGY
FOR
PEACE

CHAPTER I

Partisanship and Perspective

FIVE HORSEMEN

On the Boston Common, not far from the Charles River, stands a striking sculpture, the work of a young Polish sculptor, Andrzej Pitynski, who has lived in the United States since 1974. His spare, evocative piece bears the title "Partisans."

It portrays five men on horseback, carrying guns and long spears. The men, of varying ages, are exhausted. Though they sit up straight in their saddles, their heads are bent. Their emaciated horses have gaunt legs and narrow, elongated heads stretching forward almost impossibly beyond their bodies.

A plaque explains that the sculpture represents the universal struggle for human rights and calls the men "desperadoes wandering without a chance of victory, . . . continually fighting and full of inner spirit." It quotes the artist as saying that his sculpture is a tribute to people everywhere who are willing to fight for freedom.

Seeing this sculpture calls to mind the oppressive and often inhumane regimes that generate such opposition. It speaks of the many movements for freedom in the centuries since the word "partisan" was first used in Italy to describe volunteers and freedom fighters. And it reminds us of the passionate commitment of those who took to the mountains and forests during the Second World War. Unlike the quislings who did the Nazis' bidding, and the many who averted their eyes, these partisans had the nobility and the courage to resist. The sculpture evokes, too, the humane courage of the resistance movement in postwar Poland.

But the monument is a reminder, as well, of many other partisan battles around the world that have become so mired in violence that the original cause has been nearly obscured. In Lebanon and in Ireland, in Mozambique and Sri Lanka as in Cambodia and in so many other states, we witness hostilities that seem without end, carried on by partisans just as committed, and often just as desperate, as those portrayed on the Boston Common, driven to persevere no matter what the cost to themselves, their families, or their culture.

We know these costs well. And so we can also visualize, as if encamped around that monument, crowds of people—women, men, and children, mourning their dead, sometimes starving, cowering under gunfire, feeling the heat of fields and shelters burning, or driven to undertake desperate journeys in search of new places to live. We can see the victims of partisans turned terrorists: innocent travelers taken hostage on airplanes and ships or kidnapped in city streets, perhaps killed in their homes as a gesture of retaliation—all in the name of justice.[1]

The sculpture thus surrounded in our imagination expresses a tension regarding the defense of fundamental human values. It conveys the loyalty and courage that drive those exhausted soldiers to persevere even when they fear that their cause is lost, and their willingness to sacrifice all, even their lives, for people whose right to life and liberty matter more than their own survival. But it also conveys the risk that such combat poses to personal integrity: the risk to the partisans of becoming vengeful, fanatical, and ultimately blind to the rights and the humanity of those whom they oppose or even of persons with no part in the conflict. When that happens, their outlook will have become as brutal and as unreasonable as the one they condemn in their oppressors.[2]

A similar tension is reflected in the double meaning of "partisan." It carries both the morally neutral meaning of "volunteer combatant"—someone who has chosen sides and takes an active part in resisting—and the negative meaning of a partial, unreasoning, at times even fanatical adherent to a cause.

The tensions brought out by works of art such as "Partisans" and by the double meaning of the word "partisan" reflect a question at the root of all moral response: How can it be that people whose lives we see as precious and worthy of the fullest respect should be so vulnerable to suffering and injustice? Were there no such perception or concern that people whose well-being matters to us not be hurt, oppressed, lied to, or betrayed, moral questions would not arise. Though it takes different forms, this sense of human dignity and worth underlies the most elemental impulses of self-preservation, kinship, and group loyalty as well as the subsequent insistence in many traditions on universal human rights. And when a group is under stress, as in time of war or foreign occupation, the very compassion that its members feel for the suffering inflicted on their fellows can blunt all compassion for injuries done to outsiders in return.

The underlying sense of the worth of human existence and of the burden of suffering and injustice is as much present in partisanship as in the major moral, religious, and legal traditions. But when it comes to just *whose* worth and *whose* suffering matter, the differences in scope and perspective are glaring. Many primitive societies have a restricted view of who counts, of whose life matters. Wounding or killing outsiders may then be a matter of utter indifference—even a source of pride—unlike injuring a neighbor, a guest, or a family member. To this day, most major traditions of thought, like most communities, carry within themselves the seeds of both the broadest moral vision granting respect to all and the narrow, fervent sectarianism that leads so easily to partisan hatred and bloodshed.*

THE PATHOLOGY OF PARTISANSHIP

In time of war or other intense conflict, partisanship can foster a pathology all its own. When this happens, partisanship goes beyond the emphasis on loyalty and cohesion needed for the well-being of any community and leads people to become obsessive and heedless of their group's long-range self-interest, even of its survival. Communities, like living organisms, can succumb to stress, internal weakness, or contagion. These factors heighten the risks that the pathology of self-destructive partisanship will take over. Only with the help of strong leadership and institutional safeguards can communities prevent or withstand such deterioration.

When such protections are inadequate or absent alto-

---

* In societies that distinguish, among outsiders, between enemies and all others, killing as many enemies as possible is often seen as admirable even when it is not necessary for self-defense. Thus Aristotle held that it is better to take vengeance on one's enemies than to come to terms with them, "for to retaliate is just, and that which is just is noble."[3] To the many who hold such a view, it can seem as natural and rightful to practice violence and deceit on outsiders, enemies, "barbarians," as to prohibit such conduct toward members of their own community.

gether, partisanship can usher in a state of mind that grants neither respect nor mercy to even the most innocent victim; this almost invariably elicits similar partisanship among the adversaries thus injured. The narrowest of group perspectives comes to prevail on each side; each views the other with distrust and acts in ways bound to increase mutual distrust. Participants may have taken up the battle hoping to defend their people or out of anguish over the injustices threatened—perhaps already done—to their families, their fellow citizens, or their coreligionists; or they may have been driven by a desire to convert others to their beliefs or form of government. But as time goes on, those drawn into such wars often find it increasingly difficult to sustain full concern for the dignity and suffering of those on their own side without growing callous, even inhumane, toward outsiders. Whatever brutality or treachery they then exhibit gives their opponents further reasons for responding in kind and for even greater distrust. And as the climate of mutual threat and mutual distrust deteriorates, the chances for negotiating a halt to the hostilities dwindle.

Thucydides has told the story of the pathological and ultimately self-destructive effects of such narrow partisanship during the Peloponnesian War between Athens and Sparta in the fifth century B.C. It is a story we know well, having seen it reenacted time and again over the centuries. The two city-states were great powers when they declared war, but as the conflict wore on, each grew impoverished and demoralized. The toll in lives, and in farms burned and lands devastated, turned out to be far greater than anyone had foretold. After the citizens of Athens had crowded together for protection inside the city walls, an especially virulent outbreak of the plague brought grief and near-panic. Death was everywhere; people took to committing crimes they would previously have shunned,

thinking that they might not live long enough to be
brought to trial for them. In time, even those Athenians
most devoted to democracy and to human respect grew
capable of carrying out atrocities they would once have
found unthinkable. Polarization grew, both internally and
in external affairs; opposing parties carried out brutal revolutions in many Greek cities; and revenge came to be
more important than self-preservation:

> Society had become divided into two antagonistic
> camps, and each side viewed the other with distrust.
> As for ending this state of affairs, no guarantee could
> be given that would be trusted, no oath sworn that
> people would fear to break; everyone had come to
> the conclusion that it was hopeless to expect a per-
> manent settlement and so, instead of being able to
> feel confident in others, they devoted their energies
> to providing against being injured themselves.[4]

It would have been in the self-interest of all, Thucydides points out, for Athens and Sparta to make peace
long before this deterioration set in. But the atmosphere
of distrust had grown so debilitating that there seemed to
be no way of negotiating a lasting peace; the conduct to
which each side was driven served only to give the other
ever stronger reasons for distrust. Justice and even long-
range self-interest came to be overridden by the desire for
revenge: "indeed, it is true that in these acts of revenge
people take it upon themselves to begin the process of
repealing those general laws of humanity which are there
to give a hope of salvation to all who are in distress . . ."[5]

The ways in which those laws of humanity come to
be repealed are only too familiar in our century. Stephen
Spender describes the effects of partisanship in reporting
about the Spanish Civil War:

When I saw photographs of children, murdered by fascists, I felt furious pity. When the supporters of Franco talked of Red atrocities, I merely felt indignant that people should tell such lies. In the first case I saw corpses, in the second only words.[6]

Gradually, Spender writes, he acquired a certain horror of the way his mind seemed to be working: "It was clear to me that unless I cared about every murdered child impartially, I did not care about children being murdered at all." His perception had been distorted by the intensity of his concern for the threatened lives of those on his own side of the conflict and by his horror and distrust of the fascists' tactics. He had lost all concern for the children on the fascist side and had come to see any reference to their suffering as mere propaganda.

The French writer and philosopher Simone Weil took part briefly in the Spanish civil war in 1936. Like Spender, she tells how easy it is to become caught in a partisan perspective under the strain of daily combat.[7] In 1940, preparing to flee Paris as the Nazis advanced, Weil reflected on the capacity of violence to heighten and debilitate partisanship in a remarkable essay, *The Iliad or the Poem of Force.*[8] Turning to Homer's account of the Trojan War in order to shed light on what violence does to the human spirit, she offers a penetrating analysis of how the partisan perspective can be transformed by violence.

Weil was willing to grant that force could be necessary as a last resort in self-defense; she fully supported the struggle against Nazi Germany. But in her own life she strove to practice nonviolence to the greatest extent possible and to become someone who could make it work.*

---

* In her diary, Weil writes: "Nonviolence is only good if it works. So to the question put by the young man to Gandhi about [defending] his

She understood the contagious quality of violence, its ability to spread out of control and overpower victim and agent alike. She had seen at close hand how quickly combatants "get carried away by a sort of intoxication" and how easily they take to killing once they know that they need fear neither blame nor legal punishment for such acts.[10] And she knew how the power of violence could numb both feelings and reason, so that those in its sway no longer make room for what she called "that halt, that interval of hesitation, wherein lies all our consideration for our brothers in humanity."[11]

It is this interval of hesitation, of reflection, that permits us to think of the moral dimensions of what we as human beings do to and for each other; of what we owe to ourselves, to members of our own groups and communities, and to others, even our adversaries. In the heat of battle there may sometimes be no time for such reflection; at other times issues are so clear-cut that it is not needed; but as conflicts intensify without any end in sight, partisanship transformed by the experience of exceptional violence may numb the capacity for careful judgment, even when it is most needed and when there is time enough to stop to reflect. It is then that people become, as did the Athenians in the Peloponnesian War, capable of massacres that they would once have rejected out of hand.

The transforming power of violence has rarely been so vividly rendered as by Weil in writing of the Trojan War. But this power is stressed not only by those who, like Weil, explicitly warn against its danger. The great

sister, the answer should be: 'Use force unless you can defend her equally well without violence. Unless you possess a radiance with an energy (that is its efficacy in the most material sense) equal to that of your muscles.' Some have been of that kind. St. Francis. Try to become such as to be able to be nonviolent. Try to substitute, *more and more,* efficacious nonviolence for violence."[9]

epics sing of it; eulogizers of war can come to regard it as divine. Thus Joseph de Maistre, the nineteenth-century French diplomat who saw war as a divine law ruling the world, insisted that it takes but little time before the "kindest characters" become accustomed to passionate engagement in violence. A friendly young man, he argues, brought up to recoil from violence and from blood, can be led with the greatest of ease to seek out and destroy those whom he is told to regard as enemies: "The blood that flows all around him only incites him to spill his own and that of others. By degrees he grows inflamed and will come to experience the *enthusiasm of carnage*." [12]

For Weil, the enthusiasm of carnage is anything but divine. It is, rather, a contagious and addictive form of intoxication that injures all who come under its sway. She writes of how the embittered Greeks and Trojans, worn down by years of fighting, came to believe that liberation would be possible only through further carnage, further destruction:

> Any other solution, more moderate, more reasonable in character, would expose the mind to suffering so naked, so violent, that it could not be borne, even as memory. Terror, grief, exhaustion, slaughter, the annihilation of comrades—is it credible that these things should not continually tear at the soul, if the intoxication of force had not intervened to drown them? [13]

Here, Weil goes to the heart of the transformation wrought by violence. Violence calls out for still greater violence, not only in retaliation against those who have killed one's comrades but also in self-protection, for it helps block out the thoughts that would otherwise "tear at the soul." Like most strong and addictive intoxicants, such violence is an aid to self-deception. It shields combatants from the full horror of what they are suffering and what they do in return. But in blocking out such awareness, it also shuts out crucial danger signals as well as insights into less self-destructive solutions.

PARTISANSHIP AND DISTRUST IN CURRENT CONFLICTS

We do not lack contemporary examples of how the pathology of partisanship has overcome reasonable solutions that might have been possible at the beginning of a conflict. The ravaged lands of Cambodia and Lebanon bear witness to such a process. Israel is torn by strife over incompatible territorial claims. The war between Iran and Iraq has victimized many millions of people and threatened to draw still others into its vortex. And the African continent is beset by conflicts more numerous and more heavily supplied with arms than at any time in its history. The archaeologist S. J. Tambiah could be describing many ethnic conflicts in relating how the Sri Lankan body politic came to be polarized into two camps,

> clinging to distorted and stereotyped perceptions of each other, unwilling to communicate, negotiate or compromise and convinced that they are totally *separate* people in terms of culture and origin. . . . And the sad fact is that the main body of the people caught in between . . . are inexorably seduced and forced into taking sides as the spilling of blood on both sides heightens the emotions and sentiments cohering around such primordial theses as kinship, people, religion, language, and "race." [14]

It is more urgent than ever to look for alternatives to such seemingly inexorable reenactments of age-old patterns of conflict that lock people into the spiral of mutual aggression and distrust, and to assess the role of partisanship in preventing them from breaking free. As the means of destruction become more powerful and more easily available than ever, they enable opposing sides to inflict increasing violence on one another with no end in sight. We know how often partisanship has engendered a narrow view of who deserves to be treated justly, a corresponding laxity about violating the rights of outsiders, and debilitating effects on feeling and judgment. But never before has it been capable of so much devastation.

In any such reassessment, the East-West balance of terror is of overriding concern. Though it may have helped prevent a major war between the Soviet Union and the United States, it threatens the survival not only of peoples in the two opposing blocs but of all humanity. In addition, it is associated with aggressive economic, diplomatic, and clandestine policies across the globe that together affect the atmosphere of distrust mentioned in the Introduction far more than, say, the Sri Lankan civil war. As a result, the defensive role of these policies must be weighed against the risks that, by heightening partisanship and distrust, they will interfere with negotiations and increase the long-range likelihood of war.

Distrust is clearly prudent under present conditions of threat. Each superpower is targeted by the other's weapons to the point that sudden attack has to be a daily concern.[15] Each side is fully aware of the other's military buildup, its efforts at subversion, its fanning of third-world proxy wars, its massive arms donations and sales, and its violations—past or present, surreptitious or flagrant—of international law. Each, moreover, fears that the other aims to achieve world domination. Soviet leaders have for so long proclaimed both their aim to see communism victorious throughout the world and their belief that such a triumph is inevitable that they cannot be surprised if their more recent disclaimers meet with skepticism.[16] Some among them in turn have no doubt that the United States government harbors similar aims for world domination. Whether or not either government holds such aims as strongly as many on the other side believe, their mutual distrust on this score is undoubtedly profound.

If the danger is real, and distrust reasonable in the face of it, then how should the superpowers go about reducing them both? The task has to be one of determining what forms of distrust, based on what particular policies, are counterproductive, rather than imagining that distrust can be given up altogether or cut back across the board.

Three distinctions are helpful for such an effort. The first concerns the reasons for distrust. The attitude of distrust stems from expectations: our judgments about what people will be, do, or say in the future and about how this will affect us. We learn to have different expectations regarding, on the one hand, the competence and rationality and, on the other hand, the motivation and character of those with whom we interact or on whom we depend.[17] We need, also, to gauge how factors such as partisanship lower their competence and rationality and skew their intentions and character. One leader may be competent but wrongheaded or crooked; another, well-meaning and honorable but incompetent: neither can be trusted to run a nation's domestic or foreign affairs wisely.

The second distinction is that between rational and irrational distrust. Everyone needs a measure of distrust to be able to discern and evaluate dangers and to guard against them while there is still time to do so. It is when such distrust veers toward paranoia or invites excessive, damaging distrust from others that it becomes unreasonable and, in the end, self-destructive.

Third, and related to the first two distinctions, is that there need be no automatic link between exercising rational distrust and behaving in such a way as to intensify distrust on the part of one's adversary. It is when the two are seen as linked and stimulate one another that partisanship is most likely to reach the point of pathology and to encourage a spiral of escalation. And even if partisanship does not afflict all, or even most, members of a government, those whose judgment it distorts can carry out policies either so incompetent or so contrary to international agreements and fundamental moral principles as to add to the perception of their country as untrustworthy.

Using these distinctions, the question for each nation then becomes how best to protect its interests by exercising all necessary rational distrust, while neither succumbing to nor inspiring needless and debilitating distrust. Each must therefore resist excesses of partisanship and related misperceptions that increase the chances of irrational distrust, whether on its own or on its opponent's side; work at deescalating the military threat while guarding against failures of competence and hostile intentions on the part of its adversaries; and maintain full caution while acting so as to decrease the perception of its own policies as incompetent, irrational, or unprincipled.

But the difficulties in weighing the role of distrust between nuclear adversaries should not be underestimated. Estimates about the competence, the rationality, and the fidelity to principles and obligations of government officials are hard to disentangle. And many actions are undertaken by government agencies that are only loosely controlled; such enterprises are at times so clandestine as to escape public scrutiny until the damage to a nation's reputation has been incurred.

Paradoxically, however, distrust often affects rationality further by calling forth an accompanying form of overweening, imprudent trust: trust in the capacity of all nuclear powers to avoid the accidental launching of weapons, and trust that all who have access to them will somehow remain rational enough to withstand misjudgment even in times of international turmoil.

Yet just as we have to reject naive appeals to trust the intentions of our adversaries, so we should recognize an equally dangerous naiveté in placing so much trust in human competence and rationality, considering their frequent collapses in past conflicts. It must, rather, be a central aim of a strategy for peace to map the complex, dynamic relationship between different forms of trust and distrust, and to recognize unwise or pathological degrees of each, in order to overcome the admittedly great obstacles to breaking out of the spiral of aggression—actual or threatened—and distrust.★

We cannot afford not to try. Since the beginning of the nuclear era, distrust has contributed several times to bringing the superpowers to the brink of war. Robert McNamara speaks in *Blundering into Disaster* of three such occasions during his seven years of service as Secretary of Defense:

★ All too often political leaders and theorists imagine that policy requires either trust or distrust, without recognizing their interdependence or seeing the potential pathological developments of each. This misjudgment is compounded if they construe a sentimentalized "tough guy" image of distrust as always realistic or of trust as somehow requiring coziness and warmth. It then becomes a simple matter to expose all hopes for such warmth between, say, Israel and her Arab neighbors as sentimental, and thus to brush aside all appeals for trust. Such oversimplification is nonsensical. The proportions of trust and distrust can be quite independent of warmth or coldness. If you trust one driver or one salesperson more than another, this need have little to do with warm feelings but much to do with your past experience with them. The same is true of trusting a government to live up to a trade agreement or an arms treaty.

Over Berlin in August of 1961, over the introduction
of Soviet missiles into Cuba in October of 1962, and
in the Middle East in June of 1967. In none of these
cases did either side want war. In each of them we
came perilously close to it.[18]

The Cuban missile crisis of 1962, in particular, ex-
hibited the ways in which distrust and misperceptions and
human fallibility on both sides could easily have led to a
war that neither side wanted. Robert F. Kennedy told an
interviewer how a sizable number of the able, dedicated,
and patriotic men in President John F. Kennedy's inner
advisory group would have gone to war at the time: "If
six of them had been president of the U.S., I think the world
would have blown up."[19]

No nation wants to be at the mercy of another in such
a way; leaders in both the United States and the Soviet
Union have long agreed that a sharp reduction of tension
and of armaments would be desirable if only they could
trust that it would not be exploited by the other. But that
question of trust has always been the stumbling block—
and understandably so, given their many reasons for dis-
trusting one another and the intertwined forms of trust
and distrust.

Since 1945, distrust has also contributed to one opportunity for arms control after another coming to
naught.[20] Thus, at the Geneva summit conference of 1955,
the Soviet Union rejected President Dwight Eisenhower's
"open skies" proposals for inspection of military bases out
of suspicion that such inspection—far less intrusive than
verification procedures the Soviets have since accepted—
would afford adversaries too close a view of Soviet activities. And the May 1960 summit broke down on its opening day when Soviet Premier Nikita Khrushchev made a
demand that President Eisenhower could not meet: that
he apologize for the U-2 spy plane flights over the Soviet

Union that he had authorized in secret but disclaimed in public statements after one such plane had been shot down over Soviet territory.

Consider, more recently, two of the delays in U.S.–Soviet negotiations for an arms treaty. On August 21, 1968, President Lyndon Johnson and Premier Aleksey Kosygin were to announce a summit meeting later in the fall at which they would initiate such negotiations. But the preceding evening, Soviet Ambassador Anatoly Dobrynin informed President Johnson that Soviet and other Eastern bloc armed forces were at that moment entering Czechoslovakia. The talks were never announced; not until a year later were they finally begun. During the intervening year, the arms race entered a major new phase of danger, with the deploying of MIRVs (multiple independently targeted reentry vehicles). By the time the talks started, as Dean Rusk put it, "the horses had cleared the stable."[21]

Another obstacle arose when the Soviet Union sent its troops into Afghanistan in late December 1979. At that time, the SALT II arms treaty had been fully negotiated by representatives of the United States and the Soviet Union. It was coming up for ratification in the U.S. Senate, where it already faced substantial opposition. But when news came of the Soviet action, all chances of passing the measure were lost. President Carter describes, in his memoirs, his deep personal disappointment in realizing that the Soviet Union had precipitated "the immediate and automatic loss" of any chance for early ratification of the treaty that had been such a high priority for both nations. Carter tells of his profound loss of trust in the Soviet leaders' reliability and their concern for the peacemaking process:

> I sent Brezhnev on the hotline the sharpest message of my presidency, telling him that the invasion was

"a clear threat to the peace" and "could mark a fundamental and long-lasting turning point in our relations."[22]

The policies of military repression in Czechoslovakia and in Afghanistan were not only unjust in their own right but also inimical to long-range Soviet self-interest. They were bound to add substantially to the considerable distrust of Soviet intentions, and thus to hamper ratification of the SALT II Treaty and progress toward further agreements. The war in Vietnam likewise had long-lasting effects on the climate of distrust, in addition to the suffering inflicted on its victims. The brutality with which the war was waged and the distortions employed by successive U.S. governments to mask its destructiveness proved bitterly divisive for Americans and polarized world opinion in a way that further hampered efforts to reach arms agreements.

Much that goes beyond the scope of this book remains to be said about all these examples of conflicts nearing the breaking point or of negotiations bogged down or cut short. About each one, evaluations clash. But there can be no doubt, judging from the testimony of participants, that the distrust they experienced—often with good cause—played a crucial role in prolonging and intensifying each crisis.

The many failures to resolve regional conflicts and the overriding failure to conquer the risks of nuclear war threaten *all* peoples. Even those with no desire to participate in either local, regional, or worldwide conflicts see their survival threatened by tensions not of their making. Given that the interaction of partisanship and distrust now contributes to such unprecedented risks, some argue that partisan struggles of all kinds should simply be abandoned. But that is hardly a realistic prospect. Nor would it lead to fair results. For peoples in many nations, a permanent continuation of the status quo would be intolerable.

What is needed in response to the dangers exacerbated by the pathology of partisanship is therefore not to disparage the loyalty and the courage of those who, like the riders on the Boston Common, aim to defend the lives and rights of their associates. Rather, the need is for ways to defend one's nation, resist injustice, and relieve suffering without inviting the evils and dangers of partisanship at its worst. The time has come for meeting that need more imaginatively than in the past.

A TURNING POINT?

Precisely because the present crisis now threatens all peoples, they have an unprecedented incentive to seek joint ways of breaking out of the impasse. In the past, it was easier to invoke national or group self-interest as something entirely separate from any responsibilities to outsiders, and to argue that it should, if need be, override all other considerations. Thucydides set out the argument most clearly in his rendering of a debate between Athenians and Melians, during the Peloponnesian War.[23]

Athenian envoys had come to the island of Melos and threatened its citizens with slaughter and enslavement unless they chose to submit to Athens. The Melians refused to submit, arguing that they would rather die than lose their liberty; instead, they offered to take a neutral stance in the war between Athens and Sparta and appealed to the Athenians' sense of justice to dissuade them from carrying out the massacre. But even though the citizens of Athens had voted against such action earlier in the war, precisely on the ground that it would be unjust, their envoys now answered that they had no need to concern themselves with justice or mercy—or even with their own reputation in years to come, for

> the human mind is so constituted that just solutions are only sought when both sides are under equal necessity; otherwise, the powerful do what they have the power to do while the weak accept what they have to accept.[24]

This passage is often interpreted as a cynical characterization of the politics of power and of self-interest: nations begin to speak of justice only when they cannot get their way by force; and their talk of justice is too often nothing *but* talk.

But our present crisis casts the words of the Athenian envoy in a new light. The threat of nuclear war places us all, and all that we value, "under equal necessity." Thucydides' story of growing mutual distrust, brutality, and corruption even of the most basic "laws of humanity" during the Peloponnesian war, so often reenacted, can have an even more catastrophic ending in the nuclear age. The most basic human drive—for survival—now gives a reason even to those who saw none before to concern themselves with how justly they treat outsiders. For the first time, the necessity—the utter vulnerability—that confronts all nations equally may bring about the joint efforts and the larger perspective that survival requires, but only if governments do far more than merely talk of justice and peace.[25]

This new reality is a challenge to the conviction, as common in the age of Thucydides as in our own, that war is inherent in the human condition—whether preordained, due to flaws in human nature, or resulting from the scarcity of resources. Past challenges to that conviction, by pacifists and by those who advocated steps toward a lasting or perpetual peace, were always in a minority. But in our century, especially in the nuclear era, the search for alternatives to war has intensified: many more people now agree that humanity can no longer afford the complacent acceptance of war as somehow inevitable or preordained.

Such a search can link two long-standing traditions of thought about issues of war and peace, one speaking the language of morality, the other that of strategy. The first, stressing character and principled conduct, has roots among thinkers as different as the early Christian pacifists, medieval just war theorists, and proponents of a "perpetual peace." The second draws on the realism of Thucydides, Machiavelli, and Clausewitz to emphasize the need for competence, insight, and good planning. In our century, the first is represented by Tolstoy, Gandhi, the Reverend Martin Luther King, Jr., and many contemporary theologians and philosophers writing on nuclear deterrence, however different their conclusions; the second, by writers on strategy such as Churchill, Henry Kissinger, and many policy analysts—again, however often their conclusions differ. Whereas adherents of the first tradition have adopted a broad perspective on human affairs and stressed such values as justice and a constraint on violence, those upholding the second have more often addressed the narrower perspective of a particular prince, ruler, faction, or alliance of states. They have argued that the value of one's own survival and that of one's group or nation must, if need be, override all other values, since without survival there can be no chance to enjoy any of the others.

By now, there is every reason for the two traditions of thought to join. The language of morality and that of strategy are both indispensable in the face of the present crisis. The equal necessity that all peoples confront has forced many to rethink the traditional distinctions between self-interest and concern for others in matters of war and peace. Taking into consideration one's own interest or that of one's nation can no longer be divorced from considering the interests of humanity. And once the existence of all is so clearly at risk, it is no longer reasonable to stress moral values such as nonviolence at the expense of that of survival; but neither can lasting survival be ensured without policies that respect those moral values.

Although nations may have reached a turning point in perceiving the common threat to their survival and the need for forceful joint efforts in response, they can do little without adequate resources and models for such a task. As in the case of threats to the natural environment from acid rain and other pollutants, it is one thing to understand that the threat of war calls for collective measures and quite another to be capable of seeing them through.

Many doubt our ability to do so. But although we are still far from having a coordinated strategy and the resolve to carry it out, we lack neither resources nor models for such joint action. Countervailing forces are arising in response to the threats now posed both to the natural environment and to human societies. Research is accelerating with respect to what causes these threats and to innovative substitutes for the most harmful practices: finding fuels and pesticides, for instance, that do not degrade the natural environment, or ways of resolving conflict, defending against attacks, and bringing about institutional change that are less dangerous for the social environment. In diplomacy, likewise, as in education and social action, individuals and groups are moving to join the concerns for morality and for strategy.[26]

Increasingly, their efforts are bearing fruit. The late 1980s have seen the Soviet Union, faced with worldwide opposition to its conduct of the war in Afghanistan and with no prospects of prevailing there, decide to withdraw its troops. Iran and Iraq have agreed to a cease-fire, as have the Nicaraguan government and the leaders of insurgent forces in that nation, and the warring factions in Angola have entered negotiations. And the United States and the Soviet Union, having signed the INF treaty in Moscow, continue talks on more substantive arms reductions and methods of reducing the risks of war.

Within nations, too, the shift to innovative methods of change is accelerating. Prominent among the forces that have arisen in response to our century's unprecedented forms of violence are the movements of carefully organized nonviolent resistance reaching throughout the world to promote human rights and peaceful approaches to conflicts. Forswearing all passive acceptance of injustice and misery, they have worked out practical new methods for bringing about large-scale change. Members of the Solidarity resistance movement in Poland, for instance, have fought for freedom and human rights, much like the men on horseback in Pitynski's sculpture, but they carry no guns or spears. From Gandhi and his followers in India to Solidarity in Poland, and from all who worked with King in the American civil rights movement to the masses led by Corazon Aquino in the Philippines, the men and women who take part in nonviolent resistance have worked at achieving social change without the hatred, the prolonged and sometimes endless battling, the suffering, and the risks of escalation that attend so many partisan struggles. Corazon Aquino has put the issue as follows:

> Nonviolence is not the only force that can collect the power of the people and bring it to bear overwhelmingly on an object. Religious fanaticism, class hatred and a militant patriotism can serve as well. But only nonviolence can achieve a moral purpose without

compromising it, especially if that purpose is peace. For all its unwieldy size it cuts through to its objective with the precision of a surgical knife neatly excising the cancer from the body politic without damage to the surrounding tissue.[27]

It is by no means certain that changes wrought by nonviolent means, as in the Philippines, will not once again succumb to violence. Nor is it clear that nonviolent campaigns can succeed in overthrowing every form of oppression. Movements of nonviolent resistance are as vulnerable as all others to a loss of momentum and to internal disputes. Further, those who lead such movements to victory do not necessarily have the training or the skills most needed to govern. But examples of nonviolent resistance like those of the American civil rights struggle and the campaigns in India and the Philippines, have already influenced political life in countries as different from them and from one another as South Korea, Panama, and Burma.

One thing is certain: the choice between violent and nonviolent paths to self-defense and change is more crucial than ever in the nuclear era. For in the end it will not be the conflict between different religious worldviews or between different political systems that will do the most to determine the fate of humanity. It will be, rather, the struggle now being waged *within* many religious and political traditions. The central question in that struggle is: Must nations and groups give in to partisanship and violence and thereby endlessly reenact outmoded patterns of response to conflict, considering the risks they have come to pose to their own communities and to all peoples, or can they, rather, strive for the perspective that will enable them to envisage achieving their goals by other means?

PERSPECTIVE

> Is there space and air in your mind, or must your
> companions gasp for air whenever they talk with
> you?
>
> WILLIAM JAMES, *Philosophical Essays*

The possession of mental perspective was, for William James, a crucial character trait, yet one too rarely fostered. He saw mental perspective as characterized by "the habit of always seeing an alternative, of not taking the usual for granted, of making conventionalities fluid again, of imagining foreign states of mind."[28] No one is born with such perspective; and though it can develop with experience and training, it can also deteriorate through bitter experience and through a perverse kind of training.

Those who engage in diplomacy or nonviolent resistance have written about the crucial importance of combating every sign of a narrowing or warping of perspective. It is this effort of which Stephen Spender and Simone Weil wrote, and of which Thucydides so painstakingly portrays the failure. The same struggle has gone on in the hearts and minds of people on each side of the conflicts in every age, no matter how different the conditions.

While mental perspective is no guarantee of wise judgment—much less of wise action—some measure of it is necessary for an adequate perception of issues. Without such perception, deliberation and decisions about these issues will be skewed from the outset, and partisanship will have free play. Given today's worldwide patterns of communication, financial transactions, travel, and migration, along with the shared threats posed by poverty, disease, population growth, pollution, and war, the necessary perspective is indeed the global or universal one that so many internationalists call for. But this is far from sufficient, since world destruction can be planned and carried out from just such a perspective with utter disregard for human life. Surely, no one can accuse even the most callous of those who target weapons across the earth and into space of thinking on too local a scale. What other characteristics must a global perspective have, then, if it is to be adequate to the present crisis?

The first one is stressed in most moral and religious traditions—often in nearly the same words. The Golden Rule asks people to put themselves in the place of those affected by their actions, to "do unto others as you would have them do unto you."[29] No principle is more important for counteracting the natural tendency to think in partisan terms and to slip, under stress, into the pathology of partisanship. The second characteristic has to do with how extensively one takes moral principles to apply—whether "Thou shalt not kill," say, applies to community members or fellow citizens alone or to others more generally and under what circumstances. Finally, the third refers to the degree to which one can focus on more than the immediate present: to try to look both backward at all that has come together to shape a situation and forward at all that might flow from it depending on one's response.

The task of trying to deepen and extend these capacities for mental perspective can never, given all the obstacles in their way, be completed. But the pathology of partisanship involves a greater than ordinary failure in all three respects: an inability to put oneself in the place of those who may be affected by one's actions; a narrowing of the scope of application even of the principles one takes most seriously; and a constriction of attention to the present in light of skewed views of the past and future.

In order to resist these failures of perspective and the abuses to which they can lead, imagination is indispensable, along with the attention it demands and the compassion it can generate.[30] Without the ability to imagine oneself in the place of others, the Golden Rule loses all meaning and efforts to extend the scope of one's perspective falter. By "imagining foreign states of mind," as William James recommended, one can experience threats not only to oneself and those with whom one is personally linked but to all others as well, whether compatriots or adversaries. Imagination can likewise enable us to extend our perceived horizon not only in space—from ourselves toward the entire human species and all that is endangered along with it—but also in time. We can then try to envisage how present conflicts may affect beings not yet even born, and consider our responsibility toward the past as well—what many have called our stewardship of resources that are not ours to use up or destroy at will.

For an example of how imagination helped mobilize public opinion and press government into action, consider the debate in the early 1960s over nuclear tests in the atmosphere. It became known that after every such test, radioactive fallout spread through the air, lighting on vegetation and in the oceans, becoming part of the food cycles and settling in the bones of unborn children. Even babies imbibed it through their mothers' milk. In the face of this danger, people had no difficulty in seeing that the risk to their children and grandchildren, born or unborn, was no different from that posed to all the children of the world. Men, women, and children marched in many countries, helping to build up the sentiment needed to reinforce the prolonged and often discouraging work of diplomats and advocates of a test ban. True, they did not put an end to all underground tests, and the arms race proceeded as before; but without the joint efforts that led to the signing of the test-ban treaty by President John F. Kennedy and Prime Minister Nikita Khrushchev in 1963, the deterioration of human health and well-being would, by now, have been grievous.

Such tangible aids to the imagination are not always present. And the tendency to recoil from prospects too frightening to envisage is well known. Without continued efforts to stretch one's perspective and to learn to share that of others, the power of partisanship to warp and constrict human understanding will persist, even though it has come to endanger the entire world. When it comes to the nuclear threat, a perspective that reaches out in time and space while remaining anchored in personal experience gives a clearer, sharper understanding of the full enormity of the present danger: that a few citizens of a few nations at any moment have the power to destroy all life on earth for all generations to come.★

But while calls for an extended and deepened perspective are not new to religion or to ethics, they have rarely guided government policymakers. Such a changed perspective has seemed contrary to the short-term interest of

★ A frequent objection to calls for a more extended perspective is that it is achieved at the expense of closer ties. The stock figure of the self-proclaimed lover of mankind is familiar: someone so absorbed by cosmic good will as to have none left over for the needs of family members and friends. You must choose one path or the other, according to this objection: respect for persons is something quantifiable, unlike, say, the appreciation for mathematics or for poetry that deepens the more it encompasses.

No doubt quantity counts when it comes to distributing resources such as money, food, time, and personal attention. But the understanding of why human beings matter and why they are owed respect does not diminish when it encompasses many rather than just a few. Likewise, one can extend the concern for the common threat of extinction to all of humanity without any loss in depth or intensity. It is not at the expense of close bonds that people are likely to develop the fellow-feeling and perspective necessary in the present crisis, but rather through expanding the understanding of self and others that such bonds can generate. (See footnote, p. 83.)

governments; and it can go as cruelly astray as more parochial outlooks, unless it is guided by careful moral constraints. If it has now become indispensable, to what constraints must it then submit?

Clearly, not all constraints or ideals will do. Some are so stringent that few people, let alone governments, can live up to them. Others are expressly limited to particular nations or creeds, or to social, racial, or ethnic groups, and are thus unsuited for the collective response that the present crisis requires. A number of more general principles, such as the injunction to be more loving, are meltingly vague; insofar as they can be specified more carefully, they are more appropriate as ideals for individual conduct than as requirements in international relations. Still others have been followed by individuals, as well as by political organizations and governments, but are contrary to the purposes of making possible a lasting peace. In this category fall, for instance, martial ideals demanding blind loyalty: the motto "My country right or wrong" goes against the principles of any democracy just as, by now, it endangers the legitimate interest in survival of any nation and of all peoples.

What constraints and ideals, then, might best guide the expanded perspective that has now become indispensable between nations? A measure of skepticism—indeed, of initial distrust—is helpful in surveying the different principles held forth as suitable for such guidance. Which ones are neither vacuous, nor impossible to live up to, nor so exclusive or contrary to the purposes of peace as to escalate partisanship? In seeking an answer, I draw on Immanuel Kant's essay "Perpetual Peace: A Philosophical Sketch."

CHAPTER II

Kant on Peace

A WARNING AND A PLAN FOR LASTING PEACE

Immanuel Kant knew partisanship and the violence of war at close hand. Most of his life had been spent in one of the most militaristic nations in history: Frederick the Great's Prussia. All around him, Kant had heard ceaseless extolling of military courage, seen the young indoctrinated to accept death in battle, and witnessed war after war—now against one state, now against another, according to the changing patterns of alliances. He was scathing in his denunciation of rulers for siphoning off all available funds to pay for war, and he portrayed states as lawless protagonists displaying in their relations with one another "the depravity of human nature . . . without disguise."[1]

When, in 1795, Kant finally published "Perpetual Peace," his passionate plea for a change in international relations, he was over seventy years old. In this essay, Kant presented a stark choice for governments: they must either make collective efforts to ensure survival or face joint self-destruction. To be sure, he argued, war had long served the function of motivating peoples to innovate and to exert themselves in order to prevail against their enemies. But unless nations could now reverse course, he warned, wars would grow increasingly violent and periods of peace would become more burdened by rearmament and by hostile policies that would lead to further conflict, ending in a final war of extermination.

Such a war of extermination, he wrote, "in which both parties and justice itself might all be simultaneously annihilated, would allow perpetual peace only on the vast graveyard of the human race."[2] To the story so relentlessly retold through the centuries, of societies caught in a spiral of mutual distrust and injury that inflames partisanship on all sides, Kant could hint at an ending so final as to preclude any further reenactment. His conjecture that warring nations and justice itself might perish together speaks to us today in a more direct way than he could have anticipated. His own conclusion was firm: "A war [of extermination] and the employment of all means which might bring it about must thus be absolutely prohibited."[3]

Kant proposed a plan, in his essay, for the nations of the world to break free from the destructive patterns of conduct that make such a war possible, by deciding to cooperate in bringing about a lasting peace. The plan involved a change, over time, to representative government in as many states as possible; and it called for their joining together in a federation of free states to keep the peace. Freedom and equality, he suggested, would be indispensable for citizens of such states and would enable them to resist being drawn into the new wars upon which their rulers were otherwise all too likely to embark. Federation would be most likely to promote justice within and between states, while preserving their unique characteristics and freedom vis-à-vis each other.

For this purpose, he called for autonomous states to join in submitting voluntarily to laws they had themselves authored. In speaking of "autonomy," Kant used a concept that the Greeks had applied primarily to states living under self-imposed laws; but he brought this notion of a law freely enacted and imposed upon oneself to bear on three levels of human conduct: on the conduct of individuals, of communities or nations in their internal affairs, and of a future federation of states. This self-imposed moral law would enjoin people, singly or collectively, to "act only according to that maxim whereby you can at the same time will that it should become a universal law."[4] And such maxims could only be those which called for respecting all human beings in their own right, rather than treating them merely as means to other ends.

Only through autonomy, thus interpreted and applied, could governments achieve universal rather than partisan respect for human rights.[5] First to go, for any person or group taking autonomy seriously, would be those policies of violence, deceit, and open or secret treachery which violate these rights and do most to increase distrust, exacerbate conflict, and endanger world peace. Such policies cannot be coherently framed as universal laws. If individuals could reject such policies in their own lives, and urge states to do so as well and to join with other states in diminishing their use internationally, they could help counteract the most debilitating aspects of partisanship. It would then be possible for people to strive for justice without blinding themselves to the humanity of others, without losing the capacity to reason adequately about their own predicament, and without succumbing to the patterns of bitterness and revenge that stand in the way of more reasonable approaches to conflicts.

For Kant to stress the need for attention to morality in order to reduce the threat of war was hardly new. But it was unusual to do so both with respect to individual and to government conduct, domestically and internationally. Those who have written on how to achieve a permanent peace before and after Kant have tended to focus, rather, on one single level of conduct—personal, societal, or international. Some, like the early Christian pacifists or Erasmus and Tolstoy, have written as if what is primarily needed is some fundamental change in human nature and in the thinking and conduct of individuals.[6] Others, Marx, Lenin, and Mao among them, have trusted that changes in social structure that they believed historically determined would do away with the need or desire to go to war; thus Mao claimed that humanity, once it had destroyed capitalism, would "attain the era of eternal peace."[7] Still others have proposed a world government or international order strong enough to prevent nations from going to war.[8]

Kant, on the other hand, called for coordinated efforts at change on all three levels. Only in such a mutually supportive manner would it be possible to achieve the minimal trust without which no lasting peace can be established. Admittedly, there would be special difficulties in applying workable constraints at the international level. Kant fully agreed with the English thinker Thomas Hobbes that nations coexist in a "state of nature" in which they can call on no superior authority to impose justice among them. But unlike Hobbes, he nevertheless claimed that it was possible for them to bring about a condition of lasting peace, by freely choosing moral and political constraints and then abiding by them.

Of course Kant knew that despotism at home and lawlessness and intense distrust among nations stood in the way of bringing about such fundamental changes right away. He therefore proposed certain "preliminary articles" to help prepare the atmosphere for the larger institutional reforms and for lasting peace.* These articles

---

* After the preliminary articles, Kant states three "definitive articles" of a perpetual peace between nations. They stipulate that the civil constitution of every state shall be republican in the sense of guaranteeing

must be preliminary, he suggested, for two reasons. They cannot solve the problems of nations or of a community of nations by themselves. Yet if they are not taken into account, there can be no lasting solutions whatsoever.

Some of these preliminary articles call for immediate implementation; others provide goals for more gradual change. It is from the former that I draw the four constraints most needed to achieve the climate in which the threat of war can be reduced. Three of these constraints—on violence, deceit, and breaches of trust—are common even in primitive human groups long before one can talk about states, much less an international community. They predate all debate about more complex principles such as those of equality, liberty, or justice; all discussion of rights and duties; and all philosophical systems. Kant also stresses a fourth constraint—on state secrecy—as a way of guarding against breaches of the first three within and between governments.

Although Kant does not set forth the four constraints as prominently in "Perpetual Peace" as in other works, he

---

freedom for all members of a society, a common legislation for all, and legal equality for all; that the right of nations shall be based on a federation of free states; and that hospitality shall be extended even to strangers in at least the limited sense of not oppressing them, conquering them, or otherwise treating them with hostility. Kant acknowledges that the definitive articles will be attained gradually, if at all, and only on the basis of the trust made possible by first adhering to the preliminary articles. Yet only the definitive ones provide the conditions for lasting trust and thus for a lasting peace. Many nations have come closer to living up to the first article than in Kant's day, and we have much more experience with, and debate about, international federations (such as the UN) and the rights of strangers. While complexities far beyond what Kant envisaged have become apparent about the details of the institutions needed for a lasting peace, his three definitive articles point in the right direction. In this book, I focus primarily on the prerequisites for moving in that direction in a mixed world in which nonrepublics (in Kant's sense) still have great power.

is the first, as far as I know, to have emphasized all four in
the context of war and peace. He saw them as fundamental, however often breached, to the conduct of individuals
and societies, no matter how different their forms of government. If they could be taken more seriously, not only
at the individual but at the national and international levels, they could help establish the right climate for achieving widespread collaboration toward greater justice and a
lasting peace.

MORAL CONSTRAINTS FREELY CHOSEN

I have nothing new to teach the world. Truth and
nonviolence are as old as the hills.
                                    MOHANDAS GANDHI

Kant would have agreed with Gandhi. There is nothing new either in stressing truth and nonviolence or in the
corresponding constraints on deceit and violence, for
these, too, are as old as the hills. Every major religion,
every moral tradition, every society has recognized the
need for at least some constraints on deceit and violence,
since they are the two ways by which human beings delib-
erately injure one another.[9] From the Buddhist Five Precepts that delineate "right action" to the Bible's Ten
Commandments, from the five Jaina Great Vows to the
maxims of Confucius and his followers or the dictates of
the Roman Stoics, false speech and resort to violence are
consistently rejected. These traditions differ when it
comes to questions of religious belief, sexual conduct, and
asceticism; but they speak in unison in condemning violence and lies.

To be sure, the various traditions do not agree in

every detail even on these two counts. Some texts speak of violence in general, others of killing, still others of murder. Some groups condemn violence against any living organism down to the smallest gnat, as do the Jains; others intend most living beings; still others prohibit it only against human beings in particular or certain categories of people. Likewise, with respect to falsehood, some rule out all false speech, others all lies or, as in the biblical Commandment, the bearing of false witness against one's neighbors. All have found it necessary to debate just how to define and delimit the forms of violence and deceit that they reject and to consider the questions of scope and perspective raised in Chapter I. But in spite of differences of interpretation, the universal insistence on firm constraints on violence and on deceit speaks to the need for any community to keep them within bounds in its internal governance.[10]

Toward outsiders on the other hand, the standards have often been more relaxed. Indeed, while restraining deceit and violence within the community, most cultures have at the same time gloried in certain outlets for such conduct, often carried out by particular gods, heroes, and occupational groups. This has often been a way to channel dangerous practices and thus, again, to constrain them— keeping the violence visited upon enemies, for instance, from breaking out among fellow tribesmen.

Kant, like Gandhi, links both constraints; like Gandhi, too, he sees them as required between all individuals and all nations, not merely within a community.[11] Force and fraud, violence and cunning—no lasting peace will be possible, he argues, so long as nations continue to rely on these means of aggression. He proposes a strong and immediate prohibition of violence among nations, first of all, to prevent peace from degenerating into war, or war into mutual extermination. This is not to say that he was op-

posed to all use of force by a state; he concedes that the
recourse to force is legitimate in defensive wars as a last
resort.[12] But even then, it must be limited to combatants;
and forms of violence such as poisoning and assassination
should be ruled out no matter what the provocation. He
rejects the use of force to interfere in the governance of
other nations and to colonize new territories. Like Simone
Weil, Kant saw the capacity for violence brought by wars
as intoxicating, corrupting, and debilitating to judgment.
To him, war was "the destroyer of everything good."[13]

Kant often denounced deceit with special vehemence.
Even in his earliest lectures on ethics, he had singled it out
as especially corrupting and as undermining the precarious
trust on which human society is based. Though violence
clearly represents the greatest immediate threat, deceit can
disguise planned violence along with every other harm
until it is too late to take precautions. Lying, for Kant,
repudiates one's own human dignity just as it undercuts
the communication that is the foundation of social intercourse. He therefore sees it as more hateful even than violence: it attacks "the very roots of our thinking," he
wrote in a letter, "by casting doubt and suspicion on
everything."[14] In his emphasis on the effects of deceit on
trust, Kant was at one with John Stuart Mill, who argued
that every deviation from truth helps weaken that trustworthiness of human assertion which is the "principal
support of all present social well-being."[15]

To keep such practices of violence and deceit under
control and cut them back, however, more than principles
or commandments are usually needed. People have to undertake to respect them. Promises, vows, or covenants
play a central role in most societies, as does the related
virtue of trustworthiness, of holding to one's word, of
being a person of honor. As a result, a third constraint is
stressed in just about all moral traditions: that on betrayal,
on going back on one's word. *Whatever* principle one has

promised to uphold, fidelity to one's promise then becomes essential, and breaching it constitutes betrayal. (Indeed, keeping one's word is rarely more sacred than in criminal and other clandestine organizations, where members engage in violence and deceit directed against outsiders but need to guard against such tactics among themselves.)

The conflict between fidelity and betrayal is therefore as common in all societies as that between violence and nonviolence, or between deceit and truthfulness. It is no accident that the three lowest circles in Dante's *Inferno* are those devoted, precisely, to the sins of violence, deceit, and treachery.[16] Nor is it hard to understand why those who personify evil as Satan or some other figure so often depict the character as a master tormentor, the "Father of Lies," and a traitor to all loyalties.

In his essay, Kant likewise emphasizes fidelity to promises and contracts. Breaches of trust, he argues, destroy not only the bonds between persons but also the far more fragile ones between nations. To undermine promises, contracts, and treaties is to invite further violence, further deceit, further betrayal. Elsewhere, he links the betrayal of promises with deceit and with the secrecy that conceals deceit.[17] In his eyes, the "fawning, clandestine, deceitful enemy" was "far baser than the open one, even though the latter be violent. He who openly declares himself an enemy can be relied upon; but the treachery of secret malice, if it became universal, would mean the end of all confidence."[18]

Needless to say, Kant did not hold that *all* promises are valid—in particular, not promises to do something unlawful or to infringe on human rights, as in conspiracies to rob or kill. But lawful promises between individuals should be honored at all costs; so should commitments between citizens and governments, and treaties between nations. On this score, Kant was in full agreement with

Hugo Grotius, the Dutch scholar and diplomat, who had written a century and a half before that good faith is "not only the principal hold by which governments are bound together but the keystone by which the larger society of nations is united." [19]

Kant broke new ground in stressing a fourth constraint, on excessive government secrecy. The functioning of the representative form of government that he advocated (the only stable example at the time being that of the United States) depended crucially on citizens' having access to accurate information on which to base their decisions. Both at the beginning and at the end of his essay, Kant insisted on the need to curtail official secrecy. When states sign a peace agreement, they should not make secret reservations enabling them to fight a future war. And between rulers and their subjects, matters of public concern should be openly debated. Secret police, star-chamber proceedings, and the rigid political and religious censorship that prevailed in so many nations offended justice and allowed corruption and abuses of every kind to flourish. It was the citizens' right, however rarely honored, to be openly consulted about whether or not their nation should go to war. This, too, would serve the cause of peace; since citizens had to bear the brunt of the suffering that wars bring, they would be much more cautious than kings and chancellors about agreeing to such ventures. [20]

But the warning against state secrecy had to be carefully worded, since secrecy can also protect what is legitimately private. Secrecy differs from violence, deceit, and breaches of faith in that there can be no general presumption against it. While it is to be feared when it conceals wrongdoing, it can also protect individuals and groups from unjustified intrusions and all other harm. With respect to individuals, in particular, the presumption must be in favor of their retaining control over secrecy and openness regarding personal matters; the burden of proof is on those who would deny the individual citizen such control. But this burden shifts for governments. They must justify *all* recourse to secrecy, since their vast power to do harm and to disregard the rights of citizens is magnified to the extent that they can do so in a clandestine way.

The constraint on secrecy serves a double function in Kant's essay. In the first place, it is meant to limit the degree to which governments actually engage in secret policies that cannot stand the light of day. And second, the publicity that it calls for can serve as a test of wrongful policies.[21] "All actions affecting the rights of others are wrong if their maxim is not compatible with their being made public."[22] Secret government practices, unless they can be publicly and persuasively justified (as in the case of confidential employee records, ongoing diplomatic negotiations, and certain matters of military security), are dangerous in the extreme. The test of publicity can also be applied to forms of secrecy themselves. Citizens may well be able to accept secrecy with respect to employee records, for instance, if reasons thought to justify it are carefully explained; but they will judge very differently efforts to defend secrecy regarding the theft of public funds or other violations of the law.

Secretive regimes in Kant's time and our own demonstrate the mismanagement and oppression that accompany unrestrained state secrecy. But the Spycatcher scandal in Great Britain and the Iran-Contra schemes of the Reagan government offer a reminder, if any were needed, that democratic nations are anything but immune to the plague of excessive state secrecy. The events in both cases have shown once again how secret practices permit abuses to grow, with corrupting effects on those who are empowered to deceive and to manipulate others undetected. These practices of secrecy tend to spread precisely because they are so tempting and because of the power they confer; they add to the danger of acts of violence, deceit, and betrayal by concealing plans for such acts from normal legislative and judicial checks until it is too late.

Just as Kant saw all four constraints as necessary and as reinforcing one another, so he saw the breach of any one of them as facilitating breaches of the others. This was one of the reasons why he ruled out secret schemes of violence against enemies—of poisoning or assassination, for example—even in a war of self-defense. As for widespread deceit and betrayal through breaches of treaties or the secret instigation of treason within enemy ranks, such activities should also be ruled out, even in times of war. For a state to ask subjects to engage in any of them not only risks corrupting those who are thus made to go against their principles but also damages the integrity of the state in the eyes of outsiders. This undermines any chance of a lasting peace, for it "would make mutual confidence impossible during a future time of peace."[23]

The more governments disregard these fundamental moral constraints in wartime by sponsoring such practices, the easier it will be to do so in peacetime as well, whether to forestall attacks or prepare for new wars. At that point, they will have forfeited their own integrity and the capacity to inspire even the minimal trust that genuine negotiations and lasting peace require.

For Kant, some degree of trust is therefore a starting point in the development of fully viable international coexistence. By this he does not mean the naive trust that would invite aggression but, rather, the minimum of mutual and verifiable trust blended with commonsense caution without which the end of a war would lead to what he called "a mere truce."* This would be just a suspension

---

* Compare the function of trust among nations for Kant and in the lives of individuals for Erik Erikson. Both see it as a foundation. For

of hostilities rather than a true peace—a cold war. A truce between countries armed to the teeth and caught up in that atmosphere of mutual distrust which stems from long-standing policies of hostility, deceit, and treachery could hardly end in anything but another war.

ADDRESSING MACHIAVELLI

So far, no prince has contributed one iota to the betterment of mankind . . . ; all of them look ever and only to the prosperity of their own countries, making that their chief concern. A proper education would teach them so to frame their minds as to promote conciliation.

IMMANUEL KANT, *Lectures on Ethics*

From Kant's earliest lectures and writings on political issues to his last, he addresses what he knows to be the most compelling challenge to views such as his: do they

---

Kant trust is indispensable if nations are to control violence enough to achieve a genuine peace; for Erikson it is necessary from early childhood on if individuals are to be able to live at peace with themselves and with others. Erikson speaks of trust as an individual's attitude toward the world as well as toward the self—one that involves perceiving others and oneself as worthy of trust.[24] Kant similarly stresses the respect for others and for oneself that should preclude treating anyone unjustly. Neither writer claims that the requisite trust should go beyond prudence or call for some impossible moral perfection in others; rather, it operates together with the rational distrust discussed in Chapter I, and relies on certain minimal mutual expectations. And both Erikson and Kant recognize that such attitudes of even minimal trust are more difficult for nations to achieve and to maintain than for children, who do not generally experience the iniquity, treachery, and constant risk of assault that states have to guard against as a matter of common precaution.

work in practice or are they suited only to saints ready to suffer martyrdom for the sake of their principles?[25] In so doing, he aims his remarks, as in the above quotation, at Niccolò Machiavelli, the most forceful proponent of such a challenge. In *The Prince,* his influential book of advice to rulers, Machiavelli argues that while it is all very well and good to preach moral constraints, following them simply does not work.[26] Leaders foolish enough to insist on honoring their promises and to recoil from killing the innocent will end up tricked and defeated by those who lack such scruples.

Writing from his vantage point in sixteenth-century Italy, with its feuding city-states the pawns in a power struggle between the papacy, Germany, France, and Spain, Machiavelli has little patience with those well-meaning leaders who jeopardize the security of their states through excessive concern for piety and morality. He urges a prince eager to stay in power and to secure his state against attacks to disregard at will all fundamental moral constraints that stand in his way. Force and fraud, in particular, are indispensable, Machiavelli argues: almost all who have achieved great riches or power have attained them by such means.[27]

A prince, Machiavelli suggests, must therefore learn "not to be good." He must learn to make use of force and of fraud by imitating both the fox and the lion, "for the lion cannot protect himself from traps and the fox cannot defend himself from wolves."[28] When acting as a lion the prince has recourse to violence; and in his capacity as a fox he breaks his word when it suits his interest, and lies if he needs false excuses. But because such actions are likely to be misunderstood, Machiavelli advises a prince to proceed with all necessary secrecy and to be "a great feigner and a dissembler," in order to get away with actions that would otherwise be held against him.[29]

Machiavelli saw Cesare Borgia, with his ruthless recourse to force and fraud to consolidate his bloody reign, as a model for a prince striving to achieve greater power. "Cesare Borgia was considered cruel, but his cruelty had brought order to the Romagna, united it, and reduced it to peace and fealty," Machiavelli writes; whereas others allow bloodshed and rapine to arise from "excess of tenderness."[30] The threat of force can often accomplish as much as actual violence; in relations with other states, fraud is less costly than force and therefore preferable as a means to achieving one's ends.

Kant knows that if he wants to be persuasive in addressing this challenge, he has to use not merely the language of morality but also that of strategy: he has to speak of what works to promote the interests of a leader or a state. Consequently, "Perpetual Peace" stresses the shortsightedness and naiveté of imagining that violations of fundamental moral standards have no deleterious effect on those leaders responsible for them or on their nations. He points to the corruption and the evils that attend such violations and to the inevitable distrust they arouse; and he warns that the cumulative effects of such actions will be to undermine the negotiated collaboration that alone can avert a final war of extermination. He shows how narrow self-interest on the part of leaders, given such practical realities, will achieve short-term gains, if at all, at the cost of far greater long-term damage even to their own states. And though Kant agrees with Machiavelli that it is essential that leaders receive training more in line with the realities of governing, he insists that these very realities call for greater attention to an extended and deepened perspective on human affairs and to the moral constraints without which they will go from bad to worse.

In the four centuries since Machiavelli advised the judicious recourse to force and fraud, betrayal and secrecy, these practices have found new expression. The technology that has permitted such extraordinary escalation in the violence at the disposal of rulers as well as insurgent groups, has also brought great sophistication to the techniques of deceit, cheating, and betrayal. Wars to end all wars have been followed by still more destructive ones; violent revolutions and coups have too often merely replaced one brutal regime with another.

But the countervailing responses have been strong and equally alert to the uses of new technologies, not least in the fields of information and communication. The efforts mentioned in Chapter I—in diplomacy, as in research and social action—constitute creative answers to the increased potential for violating moral constraints. In our century, we have witnessed the growth of movements that rely on nonviolent and open means of resistance to uphold human rights, bring about social change, and create the conditions for peace. Like Kant, their members address the challenge voiced so eloquently by Machiavelli. By now, their successes provide a telling answer to the charge that their methods won't work. I considered, in Chapter I, the need for the extended and deepened perspective that is stressed by members of these movements. In their writings, some of them have also paid what may be the most serious and articulate attention to the equally indispensable implementation of the four moral constraints in both public and private life.

Gandhi's leadership of the independence movement in India is a case in point. The central element in his efforts at personal and social change was nonviolence, or *ahimsa*. It was meant to be forceful and therefore different from the passive acceptance of evil that had traditionally been associated with the concept of nonviolence. For someone insufficiently prepared to practice such resistance against an aggressor, Gandhi acknowledged that it might be better to use violence in self-defense rather than to give up in cowardice. And he insisted from the outset that nonviolence by itself cannot render a cause just. It can be coercive, harmful, unfair, untrue—as in nonviolent slander campaigns or bureaucratic harassment. Nonviolence had, therefore, to be part of a framework of moral principles, or "observances," as he called them.*

Along with nonviolence, the most important observance for Gandhi was a concern for truthfulness and truth.[31] And fidelity—to his vows in their own right, to his ideals and thus to himself, to his obligations to others —was for him what held all the observances together and bound him to them in turn. Through making and holding such vows, he trained himself to become someone who could trust himself and who could be trusted by others. Finally, Gandhi rejected secrecy in his dealings with supporters as with those who opposed him. He regularly sent his policy statements and plans to those who might oppose him, to give them an opportunity to respond in the search for a just solution. He also disseminated these plans and articles on his movement as broadly as possible in the press. This allowed him to build up a much wider following at home and abroad than might otherwise have been possible, and helped prevent some of the worst forms of repression that could otherwise have been deployed against him. Secrecy in political work, moreover, would have exposed him to government spies and agents

---

* There were eleven of these observances. Among the others were ones also quite common in different traditions, such as courage and non-stealing. Some, such as celibacy, the cultivation of detachment, and work with the body, are found in different religions but far from all; and a few, such as the home production of goods and the disposition to touch everyone, including India's so-called untouchables, were linked to the particular circumstances in which Gandhi carried on his struggle.

provocateurs, with all the smears and scandal they can generate.*

In our own time, leaders of the Solidarity movement in Poland have also stressed the moral constraints that I have drawn from Kant's essay. Their purpose has been to reflect in their present lives the atmosphere that they want their society to exhibit in the future. As Adam Michnik writes in *Letters from Prison,* two principal traits adopted by Solidarity are "the renunciation of violence and the politics of truth." [32] The insistence on both is to his mind utterly realistic. Violent resistance would most likely have been brutally crushed from the outset, as happened so many times in Polish history. And deceit undermines trust within the group, even as it invites retaliation from without. A policy of the greatest possible openness goes along with and reinforces the first two. In Poland, full openness like that practiced by Gandhi in India would nevertheless have been impossible. But the movement is far more accessible both to Poles and to foreign media and sympathizers than secret resistance groups under repressive regimes ordinarily are. And as with Gandhi's movement, Solidarity's openness and broad media contacts have helped it to gain widespread international support.

If these contemporary movements differ from Kant, it is not in their insistence on breaking free from debilitating patterns of reciprocal brutality and distrust, or in their

* Gandhi has been justly criticized for rushing to advocate an open campaign of nonviolent resistance by Jews in Nazi Germany without adequately understanding their predicament. In the fifty years since he made suggestions to that effect, those who undertake or study nonviolent resistance have been able to exchange information and to learn from one another in ways denied to pioneers like Gandhi. One can hardly accuse those who have taken part in such resistance in the Philippines or Guatemala or Poland of ignoring the realities posed by a government far more repressive than that of the British in India.

concern for the extended perspective on human rights and the moral constraints that he advocated. Rather, the difference lies in their closer attention to, and their greater experience with, the practical requirements for effective social change and, especially, in the active steps to combat injustice that their members have taken, sometimes at great personal risk. It matters, therefore, to ask, with respect to Kant's views: How might such movements and all who aim to further a strategy for peace draw on these views, and in what respects must they look elsewhere for practical guidance?

DRAWBACKS IN PRACTICE?

It had taken courage for Kant to publish his essay on perpetual peace under the narrowly chauvinistic and doctrinaire King Frederick William II of Prussia, the successor, in 1786, of Frederick the Great. Only six months earlier, the king had accused Kant of debasing Christianity through his writings and insisted that he promise never to write or lecture on religion again. Otherwise, "unpleasant consequences" would ensue. Yet in this, his very next published work, Kant denounced despotism and the barbarism of warring states like Prussia and dared to link the observance of human rights to the prospects for world peace.

It is perhaps no wonder that he begins his essay by poking fun at philosophers who "blissfully dream of perpetual peace." Practical politicians, he hints, need not imagine that the abstract ideas of mere academics can endanger the state, which after all must be founded on experience: "it thus seems safe to let him fire off his whole broadside, and the worldly-wise politician need not turn a hair."[33] Having said as much, Kant claims that he will consider himself "expressly safeguarded, in correct and proper style, against all malicious interpretation."[34]

In the remainder of the essay, he could not be farther from jesting or from dismissing the ideas he was setting forth. He is especially concerned to disprove the notion that his views might be impractical—that what seems simple in theory is bound to encounter obstacles and perhaps fail altogether in practice.[35] He intends his plan for a lasting peace to be more practical by far than the run-of-the-mill rationalizations of war on grounds of greater realism. As a result, he explores the practical aspects of achieving a "cosmopolitan"—or world citizen—perspective, of having moral principles guide political action, and of taking part in a program of gradual reforms within and among states.

Both from a theoretical and a practical point of view, Kant's plan represents a considerable improvement over all prior writings on perpetual peace.[36] Previous authors had been farsighted and often eloquent, but their solutions had tended to be simplistic. Some had advocated a change of heart among citizens and rulers, others rudimentary leagues or federations of nations, still others a delicate international system whereby a balance of power would keep war from getting out of control. In his essay, Kant responds to their writings and to other works on war and peace, drawing on the moral, religious, and political debates of his and earlier periods and on his own writings. The result is a forceful and subtle defense of the role that morality should play in human affairs and a persuasive insistence that it be allowed to do so while there is still time. In considering the moral foundation of a strategy for peace, I have found no other work that comes close to his in scope, in depth, and in relevance for our own period.

Nevertheless, Kant's essay has drawbacks from the point of view of the practical application of his views to present needs. He offers a strategy for peace in the most abstract sense of the word only. Much of what he says in his essay about the role of morality and about political changes such as bringing about a federation of states is too compressed to be practically applicable, say, by government leaders sincerely wishing to further the cause of peace.

And while he gives advice about how a national and foreign policy that stresses human rights will further this cause, he does not address the question of how peoples and civic organizations might resist unjust governments or threats of invasions from abroad.[37] It would be difficult, therefore, to derive the specifics of a strategy for peace from his essay.

The obliqueness and abstraction of Kant's essay stem in part from his background. Although he followed political and diplomatic events closely, he never had to make day-to-day choices affecting them. Diplomats, military strategists, public officials, members of resistance movements, and the many others who have to do so—all need more to go on than he offers. Even if they agree with his views on an expanded perspective and on morality, they may wish to qualify some of his judgments. For instance, they may disagree with his view that rules out as "dishonorable" all spying. Intelligence-gathering is at present indispensable for defensive purposes. It can shorten some wars and prevent erroneous information from unleashing others. Kant himself might, faced with today's many forms of intelligence activities, evaluate codebreaking and satellite surveillance differently from, say, covert acts of deceit and violence that clearly breach basic moral constraints.

Those involved daily in practical decisions having to do with war and peace might find another aspect of Kant's position unacceptable: his all-or-nothing attitude toward what he regarded as right and wrong. Though he despised political or religious zealotry, he had an intransigence all his own with respect to morality. There could, he declared, be no exception to moral prohibitions. Unlawful recourses to force, as well as all lying and all breaches of valid promises, in particular, were out of the question, no matter how catastrophic the consequences at stake. He ruled out a lie even to save the life of a friend being stalked by a murderer. To be truthful, he held, is "a sacred and absolutely commanding decree of reason, limited by no expediency."[38] On this subject, most people have disagreed with him. A lie may offer the only way to avert disaster in exceptional circumstances; why should we accept the use of force in an emergency to defend ourselves or our fellow citizens but reject deception under the same circumstances?*

It is clear from "Perpetual Peace" that Kant meant to uphold absolute moral intransigence in international affairs as vigorously as in relations between individuals. Not even national security or self-defense in extreme danger could give reasons, in his view, for breaching moral principles. "Do what is right though the world should perish" was for him no idle rhetoric. Here is yet a third aspect of Kant's impracticality: in spite of his own warnings about a possible end to human existence, he refused to believe that it might come about as a result of someone following such a motto.† He defended the motto against all comers,

---

* Indeed it is possible to use Kant's own criterion of publicity in order to show that a maxim of lying in defending oneself or another person from direct and imminent assault is as legitimate as the recourse to violence at such a time. A maxim allowing both forms of self-defense is perfectly compatible with its being public; indeed, most people would surely prefer forms of self-defense that endangered no one's life.
† Kant undoubtedly realized that the consequentialist challenge to his position has special force here. What is at issue is not only "the vast graveyard of the human race" but also the end of "justice itself" (see note 2 above). In this context, his unsupported claims that this fate won't come about if uncompromising morality guides political choice —because moral evil is self-destructive and because Providence may

holding that though it might sound inflated it was nevertheless true: it was a "sound principle that blocked up all the devious paths followed by cunning or violence." The world would not in fact come to an end if governments took such a motto literally, he argued, since moral evil is inherently self-destructive and "makes way for the moral principle of goodness, even if such progress is slow."[39]

In Kant's defense, it must be said that though he could imagine a final war of extermination, neither he nor anyone else in the eighteenth century could possibly envisage what we now know to be true: that such a war might be sudden, brief, and single-handedly brought about by the decision of just a few individuals. Moreover, he clung to the belief that Providence had a plan for mankind that included the achievement of permanent peace *on earth* rather than in some future existence, no matter how horrendous the events that would lead up to it. According to this belief, the world could in fact not perish if one did what was just.

I say that Kant "clung" to this belief, for all his late essays show extraordinary anguish about it. In his earlier writings, he was still imbued with the optimism about peace and human progress so common to Enlightenment thinkers.[41] But as he grew older without witnessing the slightest sign that the human propensity for war was abating, his writings show increasing ambivalence in this regard. In "Perpetual Peace" he alternately suggests and then doubts the possibility of a peace that could stave off a final war of extermination. He had to hope, he wrote,

---

have a different plan for humanity—are not adequate to meet the consequentialist challenge.[40] On the contrary, it is Kant's appeal to the disastrous *consequences* for humanity if nations do not take moral considerations into account that are most persuasive; and such an appeal need not be linked with his particular view of the uncompromising nature of these considerations.

that Providence had planned something nobler and better for human beings and aimed to teach them—if need be, through the very horrors of war—to turn to peace.

Yet he also held that human beings will progress only by their own efforts—Providence won't do it for them; and he feared that, although it would be best for governments to recognize right away the peril in which they were placing humanity, the world might have to go through ever more horrendous wars until one final war of extermination would be staring everyone in the face. The prospect of such a war could then *force* the shift of perspective and implement the moral constraints that all should have acknowledged long before.

Kant's warning that nations would face a war of extermination unless they could establish a lasting peace speaks to us more directly than ever. We can draw on his essay in working out a perspective and a set of constraints capable of guiding a strategy to deal with this threat. In so doing, however, we need to look elsewhere for ways to overcome in practice the three drawbacks of his proposals: their generality and abstraction, their absolutism, and their reliance on Providence to still any doubts about the consequences of acting on such absolutist views.

For a century and a half after his death, Kant's warning sounded too alarmist by far. It was ridiculed by many who proclaimed the virtues of war, from Joseph de Maistre to Hegel and Mussolini. Their voices ring hollow now as we hear them extolling war's cleansing nature, its nurturing of manliness, and its capacity to stir peoples to great and noble deeds.[42] But the strongest of their taunts remains troubling. It questions the practicality of Kant's entire approach by rejecting as sheer, unrealistic folly any effort to do away with so elemental and abiding an aspect of the human condition as war.

CHAPTER III

Clausewitz, War, and Strategy

THE REALITY OF WAR

Force, to counter opposing force, equips itself with the inventions of art and science. Attached to force are certain self-imposed, imperceptible limitations hardly worth mentioning, known as international law and custom, but they scarcely weaken it. Force —that is, physical force, for moral force has no existence save as expressed in the state and the law—is thus the *means* of war; to impose our will on the enemy is its *object*. To secure that object we must render the enemy powerless; and that, in theory, is the aim of warfare. The aim takes the place of the object, discarding it as something not actually part of war itself.

CARL VON CLAUSEWITZ, *On War*

Carl von Clausewitz, whose great work on the nature of war and strategy appeared posthumously in 1832, had nothing but contempt mixed with pity for those who, like Kant, tried to bring morality to bear on debates about war and peace. Morality in the context of war, he argued, is at best beside the point: for while the recourse to force in war can benefit from the inventions of art and science, it is not noticeably affected by law, custom, or morality. Indeed, insofar as "kindhearted people" try to come up with ways to minimize bloodshed, they can even make matters worse; for "war is such a dangerous business that the mistakes which come from kindness are the very worst."[1]

As for Kantian notions of achieving lasting peace, these too are both unrealistic and dangerous in the eyes of Clausewitz. They are unrealistic because such a peace will never come about, human nature and human circumstances being what they are, and dangerous because even prolonged periods of prosperity and peace induce a debasing softness and "desire for ease" in people, rendering them unfit for the hostilities that are bound to break out sooner or later.[2] Given the reality and the perennial nature of war, boldness is a prerequisite for survival. "Today, practically no means other than war will educate a people in this spirit of boldness."[3]

It was the true nature of war, as well, that Clausewitz invoked in rejecting as impossible the kind of final conflagration about which Kant had written: the mutual war of extermination that would spell the end, not only to both sides but to all of humanity. To be sure, Clausewitz insisted that any war could, in the absence of obstacles, develop into what he called an "absolute war," in which each side would be forced to extremes by the actions of the other. But although such a development is conceivable as "a logical fantasy," it could never take place in "the world of reality."[4] Warring nations may start out intending to go to any length to achieve a swift decision. But all too soon they encounter obstacles—unexpected actions on the part of the adversary, difficulties in mobilizing men and weapons, delays no one could have foreseen, uncooperative allies, difficult and unfamiliar terrain. Consequently, wars can drag on, cease for a time, flare up anew. They are never final; a defeated enemy can always return to the battle, given enough time. Not even the Napoleonic wars had been absolute in Clausewitz's sense, despite their massive mobilization of manpower and of national resources. And even if an absolute war were conceivable, it could never end in mutual extermination, since one side would defeat the other long before that point.

Human beings can therefore never eliminate war for good, in his view, but neither can war ever eliminate all human beings. Those who think otherwise do not understand the reality of war. The pages of *On War* are sprinkled with distinctions between the academic's simplistic opinions and the hard-won conclusions drawn from actual experience. Views such as those of Kant—whether on morality, on peace, or on war—were bound to seem unrealistic to Clausewitz, whose impatience with such talk was that of a professional soldier and veteran of many campaigns.[5] By 1795, when Kant published "Perpetual Peace," the fifteen-year-old Clausewitz had already struggled through over two years of war with France; his father had brought him to Potsdam when he was only twelve and enlisted him as a lance corporal in the Prussian army.

Later, Clausewitz fought in the war that ended with Prussia's defeat at the hand of Napoleon in 1806, and served on Russia's side against Napoleon between 1812 and 1815. He was present at the Battle of Borodino, the most devastating event of his age, in which "the inventions of art and science" helped to make possible the slaughter in the course of one day of over forty thousand men on the Russian side and of over thirty thousand on the French side. Afterwards, he witnessed the slow, grueling collapse of Napoleon's Grand Army during its winter retreat from Russia.

Clausewitz returned from that campaign crippled with arthritis, disfigured by frostbite, and resolved not to

forget the horrors that he had lived through. He wanted
to combat the illusion that the dangers of war were "at-
tractive rather than alarming"—a misconception as peril-
ous and romantic as hopes for eternal peace. In a passage
about accompanying a novice to the battlefield, he describes moving through layers of increasing intensity of
danger:

> We hurry up the slope where the commanding gen-
> eral is stationed with his large staff. Here cannonballs
> and bursting shells are frequent, and life begins to
> seem more serious than the young man had imag-
> ined. Suddenly someone you know is wounded; then
> a shell falls among the staff. You notice that some of
> the officers act a little oddly; you yourself are not as
> steady and collected as you were: even the bravest
> can become slightly distracted. Now we enter the
> battle raging before us, still almost like a spectacle,
> and join the nearest divisional commander. Shot is
> falling like hail and the thunder of our own guns adds
> to the din. . . . Cannonballs tear past, whizzing in all
> directions, and musketballs begin to whistle around
> us. A little further we reach the firing line, where the
> infantry endures the hammering for hours with in-
> credible steadfastness. The air is filled with hissing
> bullets that sound like a sharp crack if they pass close
> to one's head. For a final shock, the sight of men
> being killed and mutilated moves our pounding
> hearts to awe and pity.[6]

This, too, is part of the reality of war for Clausewitz.
Just as he rejected as illusory those views which conjured
up prospects either of perpetual peace or of a final and
absolute war, so he objected to rhapsodizing about war's
glories—possible only for those who had not experienced

it themselves. War, he insisted, is brutal, fraught with obstacles, often debilitating even to those who survive. Anyone who does not learn to suppress all emotion will be easy prey to the cowardice and confused thinking that invite defeat. Long familiarity with danger is needed, along with courage, high ambition, and, above all, constancy and strength of will, to function well in the midst of war.

But success is far from guaranteed even to an army with superior forces and strong, coolheaded, brilliant leaders. They must also be capable of withstanding what Clausewitz calls the special "climate" or "atmosphere" of war. Danger and physical exertion characterize it; but it generates, as well, a special kind of "friction" that makes even the simplest plans difficult to carry out in practice and impossible to imagine for anyone not experienced in actual combat. As dangers and difficulties accumulate, they form a resistant element that impedes activity. Just as walking cannot easily be performed in water, so normal efforts in war cannot achieve even modest results.[7] The force of this friction is increased by ever-present uncertainty—about the enemy's intentions, about fatigue and discouragement among one's own troops, about the terrain and the weather, but above all about the element of chance. A sudden fog can nullify the most careful calculations in a naval battle; an epidemic can decimate and demoralize an entire people, as did the plague that struck Athens during the Peloponnesian War; and, to take a contemporary example, a sandstorm can cripple an effort such as the helicopter mission sent by President Carter in April 1980 to rescue American hostages in Iran. Only those leaders who fully understand the role of friction in war can avoid making the kinds of mistakes that "shatter confidence" and help bring about defeat.[8]

Given the dangers and unexpected turns of events in

war, and the need to make the most out of limited resources, defense is superior to offense in the judgment of
Clausewitz. By this he does not mean that offensive war
is never warranted. On the contrary, he writes admiringly
of Napoleon and others bold enough to take advantage of
one military victory to launch yet another offensive before
the enemy has a chance to regroup. But there is nevertheless an asymmetry that favors those defending their own
territory over their attackers, in the absence of one side's
special advantages of boldness, superior forces, or good
luck.

Above all else, Clausewitz insists that war must not
become an end in itself. Throughout his book, he stresses
the priority of policy goals over military ones—of political
object over military aim. All that is done in war should be
coordinated with a view to the political purpose it is supposed to achieve. Neither vested interests, nor hatred for
the adversary, nor war's allure for the gullible should be
allowed to deflect the conduct of war from this purpose.
In a monarchy such as Prussia, the king and his civilian
advisors should not only determine when to undertake a
war and on what grounds, but should set guidelines for its
conduct and for bringing it to an end.

Kant would have been the last to disagree with anything Clausewitz said about war's brutality or about the
practical difficulties inherent in the concept of "friction,"
the superiority of defense over offense, or the need to
subject military strategy to political control. But to Kant,
these claims would only strengthen the reasons to do
everything possible to limit war's damage, especially because of the risk of a war of annihilation that might otherwise result. And doing everything would of necessity,
to his mind, include taking morality into account. Politics
had to govern military activities but must "bend the knee"
in turn to moral considerations.[9] Kant had other reasons

to advocate respect for morality even in wartime and to set forth the need for vigorous efforts to achieve a lasting peace. But his warning about a war of extermination—a final "absolute war"—was meant to speak to everyone, no matter how indifferent they might be to his philosophical views.

On that account, we have to judge Kant's imagination more vivid than that of Clausewitz. The "inventions of art and science," which Clausewitz had held to be of far greater importance to warfare than either morality or law, have turned out to bring about the very risk of total annihilation that he, on grounds of realism, had thought inconceivable.

This was not the aspect of Clausewitz's work that gained him such ascendancy in nineteenth- and early twentieth-century thinking about war and peace. Most readers shared his view of the perennial nature of war; few imagined that new weapons might one day threaten all of humanity collectively; fewer still took seriously anything approaching a Kantian insistence that governments respect moral constraints in their foreign policy. Rather, they found Clausewitz's practical approach to strategy refreshing and provocative, even when they did not fully absorb his message. They debated his insistence on war's brutality, on all the impediments of "friction," on the asymmetry between offense and defense, and on the priority of politics in determining military policy. His coolheaded realism about rhetoric of all kinds, including moral rhetoric, brought a welcome contrast to many woolly-headed discussions of war and peace. And his thoroughly nonideological approach made it possible for strategists on opposing sides of conflicts to adopt his views in pursuing their particular goals.

The influence of Clausewitz on strategic thinking has continued to grow in this century. Throughout, it has been as strong in the East as in the West. Marx and Engels studied him with care, as did Lenin. Writing at the outbreak of the First World War, Lenin cited Clausewitz's saying that "War is the continuation of politics by other means" as the fundamental Marxist grounds for judging any war just or unjust.[10] According to such a view, one need look no farther than the political circumstances and aims of warring states to decide whether their wars are just. Using this criterion, Lenin concluded that the First World War was "a criminal, predatory, capitalist war," fought on all sides by imperialist states, whereas revolutionary wars against capitalist oppression were legitimate and necessary.[11] If successful in installing socialism, he insisted, as did Mao Tse-tung in China, such wars would end by eliminating all possibility of war. Peace could never come as a result of the elimination of armed struggle; rather it must be brought about by a series of socialist revolutions aimed at securing self-determination and justice for all peoples. In speaking of the justice of wars and in voicing such expectations of lasting peace, Lenin and Mao depart from Clausewitz and combine elements from three traditions of thought—about strategy, just war, and perpetual peace—that had traditionally been pursued separately.

In the West, too, many policymakers take certain wars of liberation to be just (though often from different oppressors than those envisaged by Lenin and Mao). And while they have no formula whereby perpetual peace will inevitably come about, they, too, increasingly depart from Clausewitz in stressing the need to bring an end to war.

The influence of Clausewitz on the superpowers, along with the awareness on each side of the necessity of avoiding a new world war, offers a common background for a strategy to reduce the threat of war. If all must now agree that Clausewitz was wrong in taking for granted that a final, cataclysmic war could never come about, it is worth inquiring into his other, equally unexamined premise: that war is a constant in the human condition.

Two questions then arise with respect to the legacy of Clausewitz. Would his realism not, in our present crisis, require a strategy better suited to avoiding, rather than conducting, war? And would it not then, in turn, call for rethinking his claim that morality has little to do with the aims and means of strategy?

GOALS AND MEANS

"No one starts a war—or should—," Clausewitz declared, "without first being clear in his mind what he intends to achieve by that war and how he intends to conduct it."[12] Too many campaigns, in his opinion, were the results of blunders, shortsighted calculations, or passions of the moment. Instead, the plans for any military effort should be meticulously coordinated with a view to carrying out a long-range policy.[13]

It is in the context of such long-range planning, I suggest, that a strategy for peace can now unite with traditional military strategy. At first glance, to be sure, the aims of military campaigns such as those Clausewitz discussed seem diametrically opposed to those of a strategy for peace. Many wars have been fought for the sake of conquest or retaliation; some—usually the bloodiest and most fanatical religious or political crusades—have even been thought "holy." The goals of such wars clearly do clash with those of a campaign for peace. And yet, if we look more closely at the fundamental aims of warfare, the contradiction vanishes. Clausewitz insisted that defense is superior to attack as a form of fighting, because its object —preservation—is less costly and more likely to be achieved. But even in wars of conquest and revenge, should all else fail, what matters above all is survival, national self-preservation. This political goal of survival is common to all wars and the aim of all military strategies, just as it is the fundamental goal of a strategy for peace.

Winning or prevailing, whether in war or in peace, involves first and foremost surviving, with as much as possible of all that one values remaining undamaged. For such survival to last, winning also requires rendering the enemy unable to inflict harm, as Clausewitz insists. Both goals not only are equally prominent in a strategy for peace; they must take precedence over all others.*

By now, it is a truism that no nation can be remotely confident of winning a nuclear war; for although rendering the enemy powerless is indeed quite possible in such a war, surviving may not be. This is not to say that a nuclear war would of necessity wipe out most forms of life on earth; only that no one can predict that it would not. Because we have no experience of a war in which several nations have access to large arsenals of nuclear weapons, it is impossible to know if a nuclear war, once unleashed, could be arrested in time to prevent such a fate; impossible to know what forms of "friction" would confound and bedevil even the best-laid plans in such a case; impossible to know whether climate, atmosphere, soil, and water

---

* While survival has been the goal of all military strategies, however, it has not been central to all views about war. Early Christian pacifists, in particular, often argued that surviving in this world was unimportant compared to the life to come and to doing God's will. And that God had ordered them to reject war, they never doubted. Thus Tertullian wrote in the third century A.D. that there could be no congruity between the standard of Christ and the standard of the devil, the camp of light and the camp of darkness: "The Lord in disarming Peter unbelted every soldier from that time forth."[14]

could continue to support life even after less than total devastation.

As a result, leaders will never again be able to start a major war with anything like the clarity of purpose that Clausewitz had prescribed, or even with certainty about their nation's survival. Consequently, nuclear wars have no place today in sound strategy, whether of war or of peace; nor do world wars fought with conventional weapons. Even in the unlikely event that such a war could be kept from escalating to the nuclear level, today's conventional weapons, if used on a massive scale, would create a catastrophe beyond anything humanity has experienced. Nor, finally, can there be room in sound strategy for more limited wars that risk igniting such large-scale conflagration.

The war between Iran and Iraq is a case in point. Begun by Iraq in 1980, it was continued by Iran as a holy war long after self-defense ceased to be at stake and Iraq was willing to stop. Whatever aims of conquest, revenge, and glory motivated those who began the war soon vanished in the face of its brutality. Neither nation could have aimed for the millions of lives wasted or the impoverishment and brutalization of so many of those who survive. From the outset, the war also carried risks of engulfing the entire region and perhaps the world, whether by miscalculation or because of religious or economic pressures.

Any realistic strategy would aim at guarding against being drawn into such an inhumane and reckless conflict; the more so as each side becomes beholden to profiteers and weapons traders who help keep the war going. For the same reasons, many of the wars of punishment or religious conversion termed "just" in medieval just-war theory would likewise be excluded today by sound strategy, whether of war or of peace.[15]

But a still stronger concern unites the two forms of strategy, seemingly so opposed. If winning a nuclear war can no longer be assured, but survival remains a priority, then it makes sense for nations to direct their strategy against a different adversary: not only to protect themselves against other nations but also—and above all else—to guard against the overriding threat of war itself.[16] Against this adversary, they can still marshal forces aimed at the two goals of rendering the enemy powerless to bring about their destruction, and of ensuring their own survival. And while they cannot hope to deal a decisive blow once and for all against war as if it were an ordinary adversary, they can unite in rendering it less powerful, immobilize some of its allies, cut back on its resources, and find openings in its flanks through which to press for a reversal in its progress.

A strategy of peace directed against such a threat is no longer opposed to the wisest military strategy, including that of Clausewitz. It requires the same long-range planning and coordination of efforts as the most intricate military campaign. And it calls for the same coolheaded skepticism about the rhetoric of trust, harmony, and peace that Clausewitz evinced about that of glory, honor, and invulnerability. Above all, the strategy for peace shares the most basic goals of past strategies of war.

If the most basic goals of strategy must still be those of survival and of rendering adversaries powerless to inflict destruction, but if it is no longer possible to argue that there can be no ultimate war to destroy all living beings, then it becomes indispensable to reexamine the premise that Clausewitz, like so many others, takes for granted: that war will always be with us. He may turn out to be right; but we shall not know this until all practical efforts that could prove him wrong have been exhausted.

At the very least, whether or not this premise turns

out to hold for the foreseeable future, it is clearly necessary to combat the threat of large-scale war and of all other wars that increase the burden of suffering and of distrust. Consequently, it becomes imperative to accentuate other methods of resolving conflicts and of bringing about social change. In order to do so, we have to envision both goals and methods from a different perspective and as guided by a different set of principles.

A change of perspective, first of all, is indispensable for the strategy that is now needed. This is in one sense hardly new to strategists, who have long decried bias and shortsightedness as a central failing in the conduct of war. Thus, Clausewitz praises the *coup d'oeil* of the great commander, who can encompass at a glance all the intricacies of the situation before him. Such a leader intuitively keeps in mind the goals of the campaign, the underlying political objectives, the resources at his and his adversary's disposal, and the possible developments resulting from the choice of different alternatives. He never forgets to take into account how fatigue, foul weather, the wayward element of chance, and so many other factors can change the course of a campaign.

And yet in another sense the change of perspective that has become necessary represents a radical shift for strategic studies as they have been pursued up to now. What our unprecedented situation requires is to maintain the traditional strategic concern with taking all relevant factors into account, while addressing an entirely new adversary capable of greater destruction than ever before: the threat of war itself. Of course, nations still have adversaries of the traditional type, and caution and preparedness with respect to them remains indispensable. But at the same time, all nations, however small, however remote from world-spanning conflicts, must also share in a strategy of collective protection against the threat of nuclear war, as against environmental and other threats to their survival. Doing so calls for an outlook more global than that of much traditional military strategy: a stretching of perspectives and an ability to shift them along the lines discussed in Chapter I.

Clausewitz did not, any more than Machiavelli, advocate a collective perspective such as that which is now needed. His book was addressed to leaders concerned strictly to see their own side prevail; he drew no distinctions between their causes on moral grounds. Yet he warned against looking too rigidly to the past and thus failing to see new kinds of dangers. Were he to return, he might be harsh in exposing the stunted perspective of leaders who still carry on with partisan, shortsighted goals that make it harder to attain the larger strategic aims of survival.

Just as perspective affects how we see situations and problems, and thus indirectly how we deliberate about them and make choices, so the moral principles we take seriously affect deliberation and choice directly. A strategy for peace requires changes in traditional strategic thinking not only about perspective but also about moral constraints. At the very least, it calls for evaluating their role in policymaking and in the conduct of war.

Yet one looks in vain to current and to past works on strategy for a discussion of moral constraints on the use of violence or deceit in war. The advice with respect to each is purely tactical. Thus Clausewitz argues that surprise and deceit are perhaps more intrinsic to warfare even than the recourse to force; but he goes on to point out that large-scale military deceit—as in preparing false reports to confuse the enemy or undertaking sham actions—tends to be too costly and to require too much preparation on the battlefield to be of major use in wars. The strategist's chessmen, he concludes, "do not have the kind of mobility

that is essential for stratagem and cunning."[17] Because
cunning may provoke later retribution, it is most appropriate in desperate situations of weakness where prudence,
judgment, and ability no longer suffice; otherwise, Clausewitz considers only the immediate battlefield benefits
and costs of such action. Modern works on strategy make
more room for feints and deceit, but they, too, take for
granted that questions of morality lie beyond their scope
in this as in other respects.

This is not to say, however, that one cannot find
references in such works to the *morale* needed in battle and
to the soldierly virtues of courage, strength, obedience,
and patriotism. Clausewitz, in fact, calls these traits
"moral," leading some readers to the mistaken view that
he was a proponent of the role of morality in the planning
and conduct of war. But when he speaks of those moral
characteristics which are most valuable in combat, he has
in mind psychological traits as opposed to physical ones,
such as strength and visual acuity. (The contrast between
"moral" and "physical" characteristics is commonplace in
many languages besides German.)

Clausewitz stresses that those who lead campaigns
need intellectual ability, foresight, ingenuity, rationality,
courage, and emotional steadiness to serve their cause
best. Some of these traits, such as courage, have also long
counted as forms of moral excellence in human beings.[18]
But whether taken separately or together, the traits Clausewitz lists as valuable in waging war do not suffice for
the purposes of a strategy for peace. They serve the pursuit of any cause, just or unjust, and are as much needed
for self-defense in war as for successful assault and subju-
gation.

The same is true for the understanding of friction that
Clausewitz takes great leaders to exhibit and for the imagination and boldness that he recommends in response.

Such leaders show greater insight than most, he argues, into how the climate or atmosphere of a campaign is affected by danger, fatigue, chance, uncertainty, and other factors. They know, in part as a result of experience, how these factors hamper the actual carrying out of actions that in theory would seem to be so much simpler; and they are capable of marshaling the added imagination and boldness in execution that can help minimize the effects of friction on their own side, while increasing the friction experienced by their opponents. But because the rare commanders thus endowed can further the most brutal as well as the noblest of causes, their talents do not suffice for a strategy for peace.

Because the danger of war is now greater than any Clausewitz could have imagined and threatens all nations, the elements of fatigue, chance, and uncertainty that he saw as contributing to the total amount of friction assume a greater role as well. Whereas Clausewitz could advocate reducing friction on one side in part by increasing it on the opposite side, it is now necessary to reduce its effects more generally if cooperation for peace is to have a chance. As a result, whereas Clausewitz could speak of the confidence on one's own side as affected by the elements of friction, we now have to consider how mutual confidence is built up or eroded. We have to ask, for instance, about the particular kinds of practical problems that constitute friction in the safe maintenance of deterrence, in negotiating reductions in armaments, and in preventing the proliferation of nuclear capabilities in ever more nations. Appeals to military leaders to be more self-confident would have struck Clausewitz as an invitation to folly, in the absence of the fullest insight into the elements of friction; the same is true of the frequent calls that we hear today for opposing sides to trust one another more, in the absence of a similarly realistic understanding of how friction influences the atmosphere in which negotiations thrive or falter.

If a strategy for peace would now coincide with the deepest concerns of Clausewitz's approach, and if the time has come to reexamine his advice about strategy in the light of the perspective and stress on moral constraints now required for collective survival, then two further questions arise: What additional human traits might be required to increase the chances of succeeding? And what new paths might then open up for the insight, boldness, and imagination that he prized?

MODELS

A central element in many works on military strategy is the analysis of examples of admirable or disastrous approaches to the conduct of war.[19] They may be models of superb strategies, of armies surpassing themselves, or of great leaders; or, on the contrary, of strategies doomed to failure, of armies too exhausted or frightened to prevail, of leaders so incompetent or blind—at times so overconfident—as to invite defeat. Just as theologians and moralists may rely on casuistry, or detailed case analysis, so strategists have worked out a casuistry all their own as they weigh difficult practical conflicts—concerning, for instance, different responses to weather changes, diminishing supplies, surprise attacks, and discouragement in the ranks.

Clausewitz singles out Alexander the Great, Hannibal, Gustavus Adolphus and Charles the Great of Sweden, Frederick the Great of Prussia, and Napoleon Bonaparte as commanders endowed with special brilliance and strategic gifts which allowed them to overcome challenges that would defeat most others, and supported by armies of exceptional spirit. But he also explores the factors that can cause the downfall even of such leaders and armies. For this purpose, he often uses an example of military defeat that he knew well, Bonaparte's disastrous Russian campaign.

> When in 1812 Bonaparte advanced on Moscow the crucial question was whether the capture of the capital, together with everything else that had already happened, would induce Czar Alexander to make peace. That had happened in 1807 after the battle of Friedland, and it had also worked in 1805 and 1809 with the Emperor Francis after the battles of Austerlitz and Wagram. If, however, peace was not made at Moscow, Bonaparte would have no choice but to turn back, which would have meant a strategic defeat.[20]

Such a gamble, according to Clausewitz, was the only one that could give the French a chance of success. Had it succeeded, it would have counted as yet another triumph for Napoleon, and his every move would have been seen as expert. The gamble failed, he argued, not because it was different from similar ventures in earlier campaigns, or only because Napoleon began his campaign too late in the summer, but because this time Bonaparte had gauged his enemy's steadfastness incorrectly. "We maintain that the 1812 campaign failed because the Russian government kept its nerve and the people remained loyal and steadfast. The campaign could not succeed."[21]

Our century has had its share of both models and cautionary examples when it comes to the conduct of war. But the convulsions of the two world wars and the possibility of a third one have made it clear that nations can no longer afford gambles such as Bonaparte's in Russia. There is every reason to press the search for alternative methods to resolve conflicts and to bring about change; and the many campaigns in our century for achieving such results without the upheaval of large-scale wars and the risk of even larger ones deserve the same meticulous study that Clausewitz gave to military campaigns.

Today, a different type of leader is needed: one who can seize the moment as dramatically as Caesar or Bonaparte and who shares their gift for inspiring people to courage and self-sacrifice, but who calls for different means to achieve different goals. Such leadership does not rely on obedience and on the meticulous transmission of orders but requires, rather, the ingenuity and creativity of all who work in the ranks. In our century, it is leaders such as Mohandas Gandhi and Martin Luther King who may offer the clearest models of a creative, often transforming, response to the threat of violence, of oppression, and of war. Their campaigns have not succeeded as fully as they would have wished, any more than did those of Bonaparte; and although their examples have inspired millions, they have also been the targets of hatred and persecution. But they have shown what it means, in practice, to reach for a deepened and extended perspective on our vulnerable human condition, to be guided by a common framework of principles, and to orchestrate a complex, long-range strategy in order to achieve specific, practical goals.

Even in situations of violence and hatred so bitter as to vitiate every chance for compromise, bold and imaginative acts of leadership can sometimes pierce the atmosphere of distrust long enough to allow a search for viable alternatives to begin. When President Anwar el-Sadāt of Egypt flew to Jerusalem in November 1977, he used the element of surprise as brilliantly for the purposes of making peace with Israel as Frederick the Great or Bonaparte could have done in a military campaign.

President Oscar Arias Sánchez of Costa Rica offers a

current example of such an effort to break the cycle of violence and hatred. Joining with members of his own and other Central American governments, and supported by vast popular enthusiasm reaching far beyond the confines of Central America, he has proposed a detailed practical plan for bringing peace to that region. To the extent that the plan succeeds, it will bring to an end the brutality, the lawlessness, and the oppression that the peoples in the region have endured for so long. Even where it does not fully succeed, it will have broken through the existing despair and defeatism to offer a believable, nonutopian pattern for further efforts. In accepting the 1987 Nobel Peace Prize, awarded in recognition of his initiative, Arias spoke of the kind of struggle that working for peace requires:

> Peace is not the product of a victory or command. It has no finishing line, no final deadline, no fixed definition of achievement.
>
> Peace is a never-ending process, the work of many decisions by many people in many countries. It is an attitude, a way of life, a way of solving problems and resolving conflicts. It cannot be forced on the smallest nation or enforced by the largest. It cannot ignore our differences or overlook our common interests. It requires us to work and live together.
>
> Peace is not only a matter of noble worlds or Nobel lectures. We have ample words, glorious words, inscribed in the charters of the United Nations, the World Court, the Organization of American States and a network of international treaties and laws. We need deeds that will respect those words, honor those commitments, abide by those laws. We need to strengthen our institutions of peace like the United Nations, making certain they are fully used by the weak as well as the strong.[22]

The peace of which Arias speaks has nothing of the debasing softness and passivity that Clausewitz feared it would bring. It calls, on the contrary, for active resistance to brutality and injustice. Passivity can be attributed more easily to the many, young and old, who let themselves be carried along to reenact centuries-old hatreds without stopping to ask why. There was nothing passive or indolent about the unarmed women in Manila who chose to walk toward oncoming tanks in 1986. And the young people who have risked their lives working at village health clinics in the war zones of El Salvador and Nicaragua can hardly be charged with debasing softness.

Countless others work to further the goals of peace elsewhere in the world, through such activities as diplomacy, human rights advocacy, the resettlement of refugees and the homeless, and the protection of children in war zones. Whether they work strictly at the local level or take part in the worldwide programs of the UN or of organizations such as Amnesty International or the American Friends Service Committee, they contribute to the larger effort as well and often serve as models to those who witness or hear of their work. The men and women who devote themselves to overcoming hatred between Sikhs and Hindus or between Arabs and Jews are among the models of this kind, however anonymously they work. They take practical steps to reduce the elements of friction of which Clausewitz spoke and of which they have daily experience. In so doing they make it possible for at least some in the different groups to work together at solving the underlying problems that mutual hostility both feeds and exacerbates.

Contemporary examples of actions that increase friction and spur hostility likewise abound; they, too, deserve study from a strategic point of view to determine just how they help block the purposes of peace. In the chapters to come, I shall consider a variety of such actions and the policies that they are meant to further. Thucydides, Machiavelli, Clausewitz, Churchill, and others who have written on strategy took for granted the central role of such inquiries and referred throughout their writings to models, both good and bad, of policies, campaigns, and leaders. Such models exist, as well, for the activities that counter or promote a strategy for peace and for those who hinder or help further its aims.

In considering these models, the writings by Gandhi, Weil, King, and others in our century on the campaigns for nonviolent personal and political change are instructive. But in reflecting on their efforts, it is important to ask, as Clausewitz did about Bonaparte, not only what contributed to their success but also how they fell short, and why. It is one thing to observe such lives and learn from them; it is quite another to become an uncritical follower, perhaps a convert to every one of their beliefs and predilections, however idiosyncratic, to the point of losing one's bearings. The same is true of what we can draw from thinkers like Kant and Clausewitz.

THE CHALLENGE TO STRATEGY

The specieswide nuclear threat and all the conflicts that thrive in its shadow call for wiser and more farsighted collective judgment than has ever been demonstrated in the past. Such judgment, and the perception and deliberation on which it depends, would be hard enough to mobilize even if the threat came from some other planet; they are even more difficult to achieve because the threat is mutually self-incurred.

Reforms that could allow nations to master the crisis meet with resistance from every group that benefits from prolonging the status quo. These pressures increase the friction that Clausewitz saw as hampering any strategy. Together, they contribute to biased perception, stunted reasoning, and poor judgment and, in turn, to preventing nations from acting jointly to overcome the threat. In moving from Pitynski's sculpture of "The Partisans" to Kant's work on peace and that of Clausewitz on strategy, I have suggested the need for a sharp reorientation of priorities. To ignore either moral constraints or practical needs can serve only to increase mutual distrust and nourish the desire for yet more armaments; this heightens the risks of war coming about as a result of accident, miscalculation, or partisan passions.

The time is ripe for an imaginative and yet practical synthesis that combines what has stood the test of time from past thinking about peace and about strategy and adapts it to present needs; and that in so doing draws on today's extensive political, diplomatic, intellectual, and social resources. If the overriding aim of strategy must now be to reduce the threat of large-scale war, and if nations cannot work together toward this aim with the necessary energy and skill in the present climate of distrust, then the conclusion is clear: the most basic strategic concerns for each nation's long-term self-interest require a new focus on those moral constraints which, if observed, preserve and restore trust.

In combining the two approaches, we can draw on both Kant and Clausewitz. The realism of each can be brought to complement that of the other rather than to clash, as can the much longer traditions of moral and strategic thought that they represent. From Kant we can take his realistic perception of where war can lead humanity, his call for a global perspective on human rights and for respecting moral constraints and the test of publicity, his emphasis on our human freedom to choose to act accordingly, and his insistence on coordinating efforts at the individual, national, and international levels. Likewise, we can look to Clausewitz for experienced advice on how to carry out such a strategy despite the uncertainties and practical obstacles that are bound to arise, for caution about the risks of inflexibility, for emphasis on the superiority of defense over offense, and for a careful analysis of what goes into leadership at its best.

Thinkers in both traditions, I have suggested, have reason to view the synthesis that is now needed as a strategy for peace. To work out the full implications of such a strategy will require proposals and debate from many quarters. In the following chapters I shall first suggest, for the purposes of such debate, what I take to be the foundations that the strategy calls for and the new scope that it offers. I shall then consider the most serious objections to it in practice and identify some of the domestic and foreign policies that are overdue for change in the light of this strategy.

CHAPTER IV

Toward a Strategy for Peace

PREREQUISITES

To be effective, a strategy for peace must be capable of the widest possible application. As a result, it must set forth a moral framework that pertains both to public and to private life, that can be shared by religious and secular traditions alike, and that is applicable both within and between nations. Such a framework can offer guidance to all persons whose activities can have any effect, however small, on the atmosphere in which governments and peoples have to confront shared problems: to public officials, for instance, or international civil servants, business executives, teachers, reporters, and voters the world over.

This purpose is best served, I suggest, by stressing the moral constraints indispensable for preserving or restoring an atmosphere of at least minimal trust in any society, and therefore seen as fundamental within most cultural traditions. A constraint such as that on taking innocent human life, for example, is sufficiently familiar to members of most societies as to require no elaborate explanation. The constraints emphasized in a moral framework meant to be international in scope must be few

enough to set achievable standards and simple enough to
be easily grasped, yet also sufficiently specific to offer
more guidance than general injunctions to exhibit, say,
kindness or justice. Failure to attend from the outset to such constraints
has led to actions that are wrong from both a moral and a
strategic point of view. Consider, for example, the decision by French government officials, in July 1985, to sink
the flagship of the environmental organization Greenpeace, the *Rainbow Warrior,* as it lay at anchor in the harbor
of Auckland, New Zealand. The crew was preparing to
lead a flotilla toward the Moruroa atoll in the Pacific, in
order to monitor France's upcoming nuclear tests there.
To foil this plan, French secret agents had been sent to
plant explosives on the vessel and to detonate them. The
first blast came shortly before midnight on July 10. While
all on board scrambled to leave, a Portuguese photogra-
pher, Fernando Pereira, returned to his cabin to fetch his
equipment. A minute later, a second explosion killed him
and sank the ship.

At first, this incident may have seemed only a minor
escapade in the eyes of French government officials—
hardly a speck on the distant horizon by comparison to
the large-scale brutalities that poison the international atmosphere. It was nevertheless to grow into a vast political
scandal, rocking the government of President François
Mitterrand and forcing a shake-up in the French intelligence services.[1] French public officials made every effort
to ignore, conceal, and lie about the matter until it became
impossible to do so anymore. Whatever benefit they may
have hoped to achieve was far outweighed, even from the
point of view of strict national interest, by the damage to
France's reputation.[2]

The sinking of the *Rainbow Warrior* received so much
criticism that such an action is not likely to recur in exactly

the same form. But such actions are part and parcel of long-standing policies that are harder to change. Blackmail, kidnappings, sabotage, assassinations—these and other acts have many parallels among nations participating in cold and hot wars throughout the world. Each policy may result from shortsighted—and often, as here, misconceived—concern for national priorities; together they not only brutalize participants and bring great suffering to victims and to their relatives, but also help to damage the climate for cooperative efforts to reduce the threat of war.

Less than ever can nations afford to pursue such unwise policies. A framework of fundamental moral constraints can provide criteria for assessing these policies, and the degree to which they impair or ameliorate the climate of distrust, and thus provide a foundation for bringing about the necessary changes.

A FRAMEWORK OF MORAL CONSTRAINTS

I have drawn on Kant's essay "Perpetual Peace" and in turn on major moral, religious, and political traditions to propose a set of four moral constraints★ (see Chapter II). They satisfy the prerequisites for an international morality that can give a strategy for peace the strongest, most focused impact. Of the four, two are the widely acknowledged curbs on violence and deceit and, through them, on the many forms of harm—such as torture and theft—that people can do by means of one or both. To cement agreement about how and to whom these two curbs apply, and

---

★ The four moral constraints on violence, deceit, betrayal, and excessive secrecy can be seen as corresponding to four positive moral principles of nonviolence, veracity, fidelity, and publicity, and, in turn, to certain virtues or excellences of character.[3]

to keep them from being ignored or violated at will, a
third constraint—on breaches of valid promises, contracts, laws, and treaties—is needed.

Whether expressed in religious or in secular form,
these three values are shared by every civilization, past and
present. Any community, no matter how small or disor-
ganized, no matter how hostile toward outsiders, no matter how cramped its perception of what constitutes, say,
torture, has to impose at least *some* internal curbs on violence, deceit, and betrayal in order to survive.

But because persons acting clandestinely easily bypass
or ignore the three constraints, a fourth one is necessary:
on excessive secrecy. While its roots are not as ancient as
those of the first three, and though it is not as common—
least of all in police states, it is as fundamental to the
preservation of democratic traditions as the first three are
to the survival of communities more generally. It serves
two functions: first, to limit practices of secrecy whenever
they conceal or facilitate violence, deceit, and breaches of
trust, as was the case in the French assault on the *Rainbow
Warrior;* and second, to offer as a test for morally acceptable actions or policies whether its sponsors can defend
them publicly.*

---

* This fourth constraint is different from the first three in two additional respects. People do not experience secrecy as harming them directly in the way violence, lies, and betrayal do. Indeed, they must
often rely on secrecy in order to protect themselves from harm. No
one should have the right to demand full openness from others. Nor
can citizens properly demand such complete openness from the state.
Rather, what is at issue, in this fourth constraint, is excessive secrecy
alone.

The constraint on secrecy also differs from the first three in that it
has always been much weaker between states than within them. Democratic traditions insist on open government, but this imperative does
not apply equally with respect to outsiders. While the French government had no more right to take the life of a foreigner than of a French

The four constraints may be experienced to different degrees as personal inhibitions by individuals and expressed through custom and law in societies. International law attempts to codify and enforce them among nations. At all levels, the proportion of trust and distrust present in social relationships reflects the degree to which such constraints are seen as effective.

In considering the four constraints, some might object to the prerequisite suggested above that they should be few in number. Surely cultures require more than these four constraints, such critics might argue, and with good reason. After all, more is clearly needed among family members, friends, and fellow citizens. "Love thy neighbor" has counterparts in many religions, to go along with prohibitions such as those against lying and killing in the Ten Commandments. Thus Confucius spoke of the need for respect and benevolence; Micah enjoined men to observe "only this: to act justly, to love tenderly, and to walk humbly with your God"; and Kant insisted that human beings owe one another both love and respect.[4]† Frater-

---

citizen in the Greenpeace affair, it had every right to try to keep its military secrets from foreign surveillance, so long as it acted in a lawful manner. Yet this second difference is diminishing. Modern technology and communications systems render all efforts at secrecy more vulnerable. And the stress on verification in concluding arms agreements requires far more openness to outside inspection than most governments would formerly have tolerated.

† Kant specifies that while we owe others both respect and love, the first represents a strict duty, whereas the second leaves us free to choose how best to carry it out and with respect to whom. The injunction to love one's neighbor, he suggests, asks us to wish to further everyone's well-being and happiness; but since doing so at all times in practice is impossible, one has more latitude in what one actually does: "the degree may be very different according to the differences in the persons loved (of whom one may concern me more than another.")[5] Like Confucius, Kant claims that individuals must learn to practice both respect

nity and support for the weakest and most vulnerable in a
society is a related political ideal voiced in many communities. Why not, then, urge nations to abide not only by
the four constraints but also by familiar and shared positive injunctions such as those calling for love, sympathy,
and mutual benevolence? Surely they, too, serve to build
or restore trust.

Certainly, a strategy that stresses the need to restore
rather than to erode trust is incomplete so long as it emphasizes only the four constraints I have suggested. They
are generally granted priority, however, in law as in morality. Even someone who is incapable of generosity or
kindness toward others must refrain from assaulting them.
These constraints are only a beginning; but they are indispensable for relationships not only between individuals
but also between states.

In addition, the positive values are hard to institution-
alize even within nations; between nations, apart from
particular alliances and agreements, such values, however
desirable, can never serve as requirements. Even if they
did, disagreement would be rife as to just what response
they might call for in specific cases. Thus, many nations
offer support for the victims of earthquakes and famines
abroad; but efforts to require such support on an equal
basis from all countries would encounter great resistance.
The four constraints are different in these respects. It is
much clearer what actions they rule out. Most people recognize, at least in principle, that they owe it even to
strangers not to injure them, not to lie to them, not to

---

and love in family and community experiences to begin with, in order
to be capable of extending them to larger groups. He would have
appreciated the view attributed to Confucius, that those who practice
respect, good will, and trustworthiness in the family and with close
associates can hope, by degrees, to learn to see "all within the Four
Seas" as their brothers.[6]

break promises to them, or try to harm them in such ways secretly.

In choosing the constraints essential to a workable strategy for peace, we must keep in mind that they are to serve as guides not only for private individuals but also for government officials and all others in their public activities. The constraints cannot substitute for a complete personal morality, anymore than they can replace the principles needed to found a just society. Rather, they form a minimal moral framework in a world where many individuals and nations are very far from working out complete moral and political principles by which to abide, yet must somehow achieve closer coordination for the immediate purpose of common survival. Without the four constraints, it will not be possible to preserve enough trust between nations (or, when needed, to restore it) to allow for such coordination, no matter how great the threat they face.

The risk, should one multiply the constraints regarded as indispensable to begin with, is that they will all be ignored. The opposite risk is equally great: of acknowledging no moral limitations at all—thinking it sufficient, perhaps, to rely solely on what one takes to be one's common sense, or the welfare of one's client, company, or nation; or, for that matter, on one's love for mankind. Those who give themselves such leeway from specific constraints assume, rashly, that they need no internal compass to compensate for their own errors and biases. As soon as they skip past ordinary requirements for justifying their choices, they open themselves to the risks of partisanship and often end by condoning abuses for the sake of their particular cause or ideal.

Not only are the four constraints indispensable separately; they must also be seen as linked. All talk of morality that focuses only on one value at the expense of others risks collapsing into moralizing of the most dangerous

kind: the trampling on fundamental moral principles in
the name of promoting some particular ideal or combating
some particular evil (see Chapter V). The remedy lies in
seeing the four basic moral constraints as *forming a framework* and as thereby both limiting and enhancing one another. In this framework, the constraint on betrayal
buttresses those on violence and on deceit, while the limit
on excessive secrecy prevents abuses of the first three.

With respect to this framework, another question
may arise. Why not see the constraint on violence as foremost in the context of war and peace, with the other three
shoring it up? What nations fear most is surely the violence
of invasions, of bombardments and the laying waste of
cities and countryside. I would agree that the goal of the
framework of constraints is indeed to forestall such violence in the first place. The constraint on violence clearly
has the most direct bearing on that goal, but it is also
needed, along with the other three, to rule out actions that
erode trust and increase the threat of war—sabotage or
assassination, say, or cheating on arms treaties. The four
are then equally important. If you cannot trust a government's pledge or treaty of nonaggression, then you can
have no trust that it will refrain from such aggression.

A further objection may be raised with respect to the
requirements that the constraints chosen should be simple
enough to be easily grasped and specific enough to offer
practical guidance. For although the four constraints do
satisfy these requirements in principle and often also in
practice, their applications are not simple to work out in
situations where they conflict or appear to do so. This is a
valid objection to any attempt to suggest constraints easily
applicable to all possible conflicts. But it does not invali-
date the present effort to set forth the constraints most
needed in a strategy for peace. Such a strategy cannot
aspire to resolve all existing moral dilemmas. Rather, so
long as it offers specific guidance in clear-cut cases and

succeeds in reducing the number of conflicts that are more resistant to efforts at principled resolution, it will make considerable progress in reducing distrust.

In order to cut back the number of these conflicts, it is indispensable, first of all, to recognize exceptions to the moral constraints selected. They must be seen as strict without being unconditional. Yet how can one allow such a modification, an absolutist like Kant might ask, without compromising the very notion of a framework of moral constraints? Certain acts, even if carried out under duress, are such as to destroy a person's integrity and self-respect; once people allow for even a few exceptions to moral principles they can slip into every form of abuse and mis-judgment, the more easily if their judgment is skewed by partisanship. As Kant pointed out, unless we take moral principles to be absolutely binding at all times, we are especially likely to make an exception just for ourselves and "just for this once." [7]

These warnings should carry great weight for anyone who considers violating a moral constraint. But it would be self-defeating for a strategy aimed at reducing the chances of a nuclear catastrophe to insist on hewing to principle even at the cost of making just such a disaster more likely. Less than ever, in the nuclear era, can we afford to hold, with Kant, that one should "do what is right though the world might perish"—refuse to tell a lie, say, even to a band of nuclear terrorists in order to keep them from precipitating a global catastrophe.* Kant but-

---

* In agreeing that the stringency of moral constraints must at times be limited by the expected consequences of actions and practices, I join company, at least in this respect, with John Stuart Mill and other con-sequentialists. But it is worth noting that, although the theories of Kant and Mill differ with respect to the role of consequences, the practical choices that they advocate are often quite similar. Thus, Mill insisted on the importance of preserving a climate of trust, in which there should be few exceptions to principles of truthfulness, nonviolence,

tressed his absolutist claim by relying on what he admitted was no more than a hope: that Providence would keep the world from perishing. Yet to gamble on being rescued by Providence in our present circumstances would be far too casual. It is noteworthy, in this respect, that the American Catholic bishops and other religious groups that have contributed so forcefully to the debate about war and peace in recent years have, to the best of my knowledge, consistently steered clear of such an assumption.[9]

"Do what is right though the heavens should fall" still guides some, who regard such a maxim as divinely ordained and are willing to suffer the consequences for the sake of their faith.[10] But they cannot demand that those who disagree with their religious beliefs should nevertheless accept their uncompromising maxim. It cannot serve as a universal precept in the nuclear era and would find few adherents among public officials responsible for choices involving life or death.

The desire for absolute certainty about every issue of right and wrong is tempting in theory but can never be satisfied in practice. Even those who grant no exceptions to certain prohibitions still have to draw lines with respect to what should count as falling within the prohibited category.[11] If they rule out, say, all killing, do they mean to

---

and promise-keeping.[8] And by defining and analyzing practical problems, Kant often used all his ingenuity to respond so as to neither breach moral principles nor cause undesirable consequences. When it comes to choice in the face of nuclear devastation, Kantian and consequentialist approaches, along with those of natural law and most other moral traditions, would, I believe, all accept the need for an extended perspective, a framework of moral constraints, and a practical approach to implementing them. (This is not to say, however, that different interpretations of the dangers at issue, of what moral considerations apply, and of the potential consequences of alternative strategies do not diverge in the present debate.)

prohibit capital punishment and the killing of animals? Or are they speaking, rather, about the killing of innocent human beings? If so, how do they categorize noncombatants in war? And can they always be sure who is and who is not a noncombatant? Between nations, do they rule out even the killing that takes place in wars of strict self-defense? If not, how do they draw the line, among all the wars that states brazenly claim are strictly in self-defense, between those that are genuinely such and all the other ones? And regardless of how they come out on all these questions, how do they classify policies or acts that, while not directly taking lives, place large numbers of people at risk of near-certain death? Moderate risk? Indeterminate risk? In all such cases, line-drawing will still be needed, no matter how rigidly moral rules may be defined.

Similarly, problems of line-drawing come up for anyone who admits exceptions to moral constraints. It then becomes necessary to weigh marginally different cases and to ask how clear it is that a particular action qualifies as an exception, and on what grounds. If you have concluded, for example, that it is legitimate to lie to deflect a would-be assassin on the trail of an intended victim, what about those borderline cases in which you are not sure of the pursuer's intention or of his capacity to carry it out? How do you demarcate the kinds of cases where you take lies to be justified from among the many marginally different cases where you are no longer sure?

LINE-DRAWING

The effort to perceive distinctions and to draw lines between different actions, plans, and characteristics lies at the core of practical choice, whether in legal, religious, or moral contexts. While an area of uncertainty or dispute about difficult cases will always remain, such an effort can reduce it considerably.*

To see how questions of line-drawing arise in practice, consider, once again, the French sabotage of the *Rainbow Warrior*. Those who sponsored this venture might agree that it is generally wrong to sink foreign vessels in peacetime and to take human lives in the process. But in this instance, the French officials might argue, the assault was a clear case of self-defense. In their view, members of the Greenpeace organization threatened France's military preparedness by their insistence on observing its nuclear tests. The government had tried every legal means of stopping such observations, to no avail. And while the action presented serious risks to those on board the vessel, no violence toward any individual had been intended, given the warning blasts meant to frighten all on board into disembarking.

These arguments might well appear less persuasive to the officials who planned the sabotage if environmentalists were to take similar liberties with the property and the lives of French citizens. That question took on practical significance a year later, when Paul Watson, reportedly expelled from Greenpeace in 1977 and the leader of another environmental group, the Shepherds of the Sea, claimed responsibility for sinking two of Iceland's four

---

* Thinkers in the great traditions of practical moral inquiry—among them Confucians, Stoics, and commentators on Christian, Jewish, Buddhist, and Islamic ethics—have developed methods of sorting through moral problems that can illuminate many of the difficulties that still confront us today. They have discussed the ways in which particular choices and ways of leading one's life interact; considered the role played by definitions and different forms of justification; explored the nature of analogies and the relationship between principle and practice; and worked out methods of line-drawing in difficult cases of conflict that distinguish between marginally different definitions, circumstances, and degrees of justification.

whaling ships. He argued that his followers had used no explosives and been careful to avoid any loss of life. They had begun opening key valves in the ships only when they had ascertained that the entire crew had left each ship; and they claimed that such destruction of property did not constitute violence. Illegal acts, Mr. Watson is reported to have said, are justified to stop environmental abuse, as long as they defend and do not endanger living things: but "people tend to have more respect for private property than for the sanctity of life."[12]

The Greenpeace organization, though its representatives have long urged an end to whale hunting, denounced such methods of aggression, whether to property or to life. We see, then, three different lines drawn to define what one can rightly do to those regarded as adversaries on a political issue: one line rejects all action meant to injure life or property; a second rejects posing direct risks to life but not destroying property; and a third allows placing lives at risk as well as destroying property. It is possible to envisage any number of additional cases incrementally more or less violent and/or destructive than the attack on the *Rainbow Warrior* or of the Icelandic whaling ships. Likewise, one can imagine different degrees of justification for the acts, ranging from self-defense in an imminent national emergency to sheer aggression for its own sake.

Line-drawing, in these cases as in many others, is both unavoidable and open to different forms of error and bias. States, like individuals, define themselves and the integrity they strive for in part through the lines that they draw in principle and the degree to which they honor these lines in practice.

That task is never entirely completed; new cases and new circumstances arise to test boundaries that once seemed clear. To take an analogy from medicine: up to this century, it was usually easy for doctors to state whether a person had died or was still alive. With the advent of modern technology allowing them to keep a patient's heart beating even though the brain may have ceased functioning, physicians and legislatures have had to draw new lines with respect to when death has arrived. In most cases, doctors can still diagnose death as readily as in the past; but there are now different types of borderline cases where complete certainty eludes them and a few where sharp moral disagreement persists. Similarly, technology has made it possible for states to threaten and to spy upon each other in new ways; and the questions raised by these developments have brought disagreement as intense as that associated with the end of life.

How might policymakers best approach the task of establishing standards and making choices, given these difficulties? It helps to start out with a shared framework of moral constraints and to formulate clear-cut cases to which all agree that the constraints apply; from such a basis, it is easier to explore remaining differences. For this purpose, one can envisage certain examples of clearly unjustifiable or, on the contrary, clearly justifiable instances of violence, deceit, breaches of faith, or secrecy, as benchmarks.

Terrorism, for instance, is clearly unjustifiable from the point of view of such a framework of constraints. One need not attempt to draw lines with respect to acts of threatening or engaging in violence against civilians, often randomly, so as to spread terror and thereby to further political aims. Such acts are wholly on one side of the line —the side that should be ruled out. Ruling out terrorist practices, however, will call for more than the customary denunciation, the more so as many leaders publicly reject such practices while engaging in them, subsidizing them, or tolerating them in secret. Partisanship leads some to justify terrorist action by those on their own side on the ground that they are freedom fighters while castigating their opponents as terrorists pure and simple. Yet all who place bombs on buses or planes, say, or strafe health clinics or schools, must be seen as terrorists, however dedicated they may be to the cause of freedom. Governments likewise engage in terror if they resort to such methods at home or abroad, no matter how noble the purposes they claim to serve.

Disinformation is another practice that can serve as a benchmark when it comes to violating a fundamental moral constraint. For while one may debate where to draw the line when it comes to different items of deceptive propaganda, depending on how clearly they are intended to deceive and the degree to which they depart from the truth, no such debates need arise over schemes of disinformation; they are planned from the outset to mislead, whether by means of planting false information in the press, forging documents, or inducing officials to give false testimony.

Terrorism and disinformation, and related forms of violence and deceit, not only wreak scatter-shot injury on victims; they also hurt the credibility and the reputation of governments and organizations known to engage in them, damaging the atmosphere in which nations must try to work out responses to the overriding collective threat of war. Once set, such examples of disrespect for law and morality linger long after particular incidents have ceased to dominate newspaper headlines. Such policies invite retaliation and imitation on the part of adversaries and add to public distrust, especially among citizens made complicitous against their will.

With such benchmarks in mind, it becomes easier to separate clear-cut cases from the rest and to determine where, along such different dimensions as that of the degree of violence or the innocence of the victims, uncertainty and disagreement arise. Much of what human beings do—governments as well as private groups and individuals—is perfectly consonant with the four constraints and thus unproblematic from those points of view. Of the types of conduct that do violate the constraints, a small number are within the range of justifiable breaches, while most are clearly illegitimate.

As for cases where there is more disagreement even in principle about how to evaluate them, what might be entailed by deliberating about them? In earlier writings, I have suggested a three-step procedure for weighing an action or a practice fraught with conflict: first, to ask whether there is an alternative course of action that will achieve the aims one takes to be good without breaching moral constraints; second, if one sees no such alternative, to set forth the moral arguments thought to excuse or to justify such breaches, along with possible counterarguments; and third, in weighing them, and as a test of the first two steps, to ask how such arguments would fare if defended in front of an assembly of reasonable critics.[13]

How does this three-step procedure apply in the case of the *Rainbow Warrior* or the activities of the Shepherds of the Sea? Those responsible for both actions argued that they chose to act as they did only after having exhausted all lawful means at their disposal. But even if such a claim is accurate, it is not, by itself, sufficient to justify peacetime assaults on civilians or their property. If government officials explained that they had tried every lawful means of raising funds needed to support a friendly regime in distress, and that they had turned to extortion for this worthy cause only when all else failed, they would not expect to persuade many.

Nor does the moral deliberation called for in the second step justify the French action or that of the Shepherds.

France's long-range aim of enhancing national security by preventing observation of her nuclear tests might justify restricting access to the test site but not sinking ships and taking human lives. The Shepherds argued that their assault was called for in defense of innocent lives otherwise at risk—an argument also advanced by those who place explosives in abortion clinics. Among the many groups likewise invoking the defense of innocent lives or national security for their violations of clear-cut moral standards, few go beyond such rationales to examine the impact of their actions on those whom they injure indirectly, on themselves as moral agents, or on their societies. Nor do they consider the moral relevance of inviting, through their conduct, further retaliation by their adversaries and imitation by yet other groups with different agendas, equally passionately held, or the cumulative effect on the climate of distrust within or between communities.

In making such arguments, while shunting aside all but the narrowest considerations, those planning to violate moral constraints often take for granted that these constraints should nonetheless hold for others. Yet the question, What if everybody did that? is in part meant to expose the inadequacy, in the absence of further arguments, of such self-serving exceptions.

The reasons offered in support of violations are especially likely to remain inchoate and partisan so long as they are not open to challenge from the outside. The third step, the test of publicity, is meant to provide such a challenge. It helps counteract biases, errors, and ignorance—and thus the misjudgments they bring about—by asking how justifications and excuses would hold up in open debate and what would happen if, as often occurs, those responsible for planning, authorizing, and carrying out clandestine actions were exposed to public criticism.

When it comes to government policies in a democracy, the test of publicity requires full accountability to the public or to their elected representatives.[14] By making one's arguments explicit and subjecting them to inspection and criticism, the test challenges private biases, errors, and ignorance, and allows the stretching of perspective so crucial to moral choice. Such sensitivity is never more important than when distrust between adversary groups is strong and partisanship risks skewing their judgment.

The three-step procedure may turn out not to be needed in clear-cut cases. And it can rarely bring a fully satisfactory resolution to the most difficult conflicts—least of all to what have come to be known as "tragic conflicts," in which the available alternatives are all dismal from a moral point of view. In *Mortal Questions,* the philosopher Thomas Nagel asks about such a situation: "What if the world itself, or someone else's actions, could face a previously innocent person with a choice between two morally abominable courses of action, and leave him no way to escape with his honor?"[15]* An officer may be ordered to torture terrorists to learn where they have concealed the bombs with which they are threatening to blow up a city; a government leader may have to choose between violating a binding treaty and risking full-scale war.

But such conflicts are rare. Good government can make them rarer still. Most of the time, government officials as well as private individuals know quite well when injunctions such as those not to kill or to lie bear upon

---

* Though such choices are stark ones, questions of line-drawing may nevertheless be at issue for those having to arrive at a decision. If they consider doing nothing rather than choosing one of two or more such "abominable choices," they may ask themselves how great the likely harm must be before they change their minds and choose the lesser evil. And if they cannot avoid choosing one of the evils, say, because they are threatened at gunpoint, how do they compare the kinds and amounts of harm that they will produce?

their actions. As a result, I shall argue that we can get off to a good start with a strategy for peace merely by cutting back on activities that clearly violate the most fundamental moral standards—rejecting all support for terrorism, torture, assassination, disinformation, cheating on arms agreements, and the mining of harbors and international waterways, for instance—and by encouraging policies that restore, rather than damage, confidence between nations.

Even with respect to marginally legitimate activities —say, ones that come close to involving treaty violations —it matters that governments bend over backwards to avoid them when at all possible. Such acts are peculiarly open to misinterpretation and to charges of hypocrisy. They create precedents, habits, and policies that can lead to more flagrant abuses. They then combine with the clear-cut violations to increase distrust of a government among other nations and to add to the cynicism and discouragement among its own citizens. The more discredited a government has become, the greater are the difficulties that it will experience in regaining respect. For all these reasons, those who advocate or take part in practices that risk violating fundamental moral constraints should assume that they confront a heavy burden of proof.

Putting into practice a framework of moral constraints does not call for agreement on all questions still in dispute. If it did, the urgent work for peace would never begin. Rather, it calls for agreement about clear-cut practices and for working one's way toward resolution of those about which there is still widespread disagreement. It is in such practical ways that the strategy for peace can be undertaken. Focusing on the aim of collective survival, cognizant of the resources it must mobilize and of the obstacles it confronts, holding to the framework of fundamental moral principles that restricts some means and encourages others, such a strategy can serve to unite many disparate efforts to reduce the threat of war.

NEW SCOPE FOR STRATEGY

If a strategy for peace is to be as widely implemented as possible, its scope must be broad, the more so as the obstacles to achieving a lasting peace have themselves grown so formidable. The world's population has gone from around one billion to around five billion in the two hundred years since Kant wrote, adding to the pressures for resources and territory, and may double again in the next fifty years. The toll from war and famine has likewise multiplied. Although international organizations are playing a growing role in our century, they have no means, as yet, for bringing an end to the many wars that continue to plague so many regions, or for coping with the risks from modern weapons.

Without more extensive scope for a strategy for peace, these obstacles may deflect all efforts at fundamental change, given the prevailing climate of distrust among nations. To provide greater scope, I would like to suggest the need for emphasizing and combining two modern developments of strategic thinking, increasingly recognized by Eastern as well as Western nations. The first development extends the concept of "strategy" to encompass all that a nation does that affects its relations with other nations. The second is that of "confidence-building measures" agreed upon by governments in order to reduce the risk of surprise attacks or confrontations arising out of miscalculation.[16]

The first approach, now common to many nations, takes strategy to have far greater reach than in the past.

This is in part because war, in the twentieth century, has come to be waged not merely through military but also through political, diplomatic, psychological, and economic action. The tactics of war and peace are now less clearly separated than in the past; strategy therefore includes many activities beyond the strictly military and extends to periods of peace as well as of war. Accordingly, "strategy" is defined by the U.S. Joint Chiefs of Staff, as

> the art and science of developing and using political, economic, psychological and military forces as necessary during peace and war, to afford the maximum support to policies, in order to increase the probabilities and favorable consequences of victory and to lessen the changes of defeat.[17]

All that a nation does, not only with a view to surviving but to thriving economically and politically, is explicitly part of strategy thus conceived. Some governments conduct economic warfare by every means short of military occupation, including blockade, large-scale technological theft, dumping, and economic penetration. Similarly, operations of psychological warfare may go all the way from the mildest propaganda to forgery, disinformation, and vilification campaigns. And when leaders sponsor guerilla wars against nations with which they are nominally at peace, the lines between wartime and peacetime activities are hard to draw.[18]

With two obvious qualifications, the strategy for peace that I propose can accept and indeed embrace the broad definition offered by the Joint Chiefs of Staff:

—strategy *ought* to partake of "art" as well as of "science";
—it *ought* to use "political, economic, psychological and military forces" and do so "during peace and war";

—and its purpose *should* be "to increase the probabilities
and favorable consequences of victory and to lessen the
chances of defeat."

The vital qualifications that we must add have to do
with the end—victory—and the means of such an expanded strategy. The necessary victory is no longer only
over adversaries in particular conflicts but over the threat
of large-scale war itself. And in order to reduce that threat
and bring peace to regions now at war, the means employed must respect a framework of moral constraints—
not merely in wartime but, most urgently, before actual
war breaks out.

The second contemporary approach to strategy, that
of "confidence-building measures," accords with such a
framework of constraints; but it lacks, as yet, a sufficiently
broad perspective. An agreement signed at a thirty-five-
nation conference on September 22, 1986, in Stockholm,
contains a number of clauses meant to reduce the risk of
needless provocation and accidental war. In particular, the
signatories pledged that any state planning to carry out
military exercises in Europe or to undertake troop movements in ways that might appear threatening would
announce such plans in advance and accept mandatory
on-site inspection.

All parties stand to gain from signing such a treaty.
It threatens no one; and no nation wants to be drawn
into war because of an avoidable failure to account
for military movements. The agreement breaks new
ground, however, in allowing openness in these
matters between nations and in recognizing that
building trust in such ways reduces the tensions that
can lead to war. It presupposes not only openness in certain limited and carefully specified ways but also full
observance, in these respects, of the other three constraints that are part of the framework I have proposed:

nonviolence, veracity, and respect for treaties and commitments.

If, however, any nation signs such an agreement only to ignore it by breaching its provisions, it will increase rather than decrease the burden of distrust in international relations. Treaty-breaking is, here as always, of special importance in its corrosive effect on trust. Agreeing to give notice of troop movements, for example, only to proceed not to do so, will arouse greater distrust than would a refusal to give such notice in the first place. A nation that acts thus with respect to confidence-building measures will be less trusted in other negotiations as well.[19] As a result, the framework of moral constraints, and especially the constraints on deception, breaches of faith, and secrecy, can be of use only if they are taken seriously by all parties to such a treaty from the beginning.

To the extent that nations realize that their self-interest requires them to adhere to the Stockholm treaty, therefore, they will have made a good beginning. But the treaty is still no more than a beginning. It has addressed a few issues clearly of interest to all parties in the East-West conflict and thus in the interest of all nations now at risk through that conflict. But it has focused only on the European theater and, even in that limited context, only on a few types of military maneuvers.

How might the concept of confidence-building measures be enlarged? I suggest that we view it provisionally from the expansive perspective on strategy discussed earlier and aim to extend the measures gradually beyond the Stockholm agreement in five ways:

1. *Over time, similar agreements should be negotiated for measures that apply not only to Europe but to every region in the world.* All nations facing actual or potential conflicts would benefit from measures to reduce the likelihood of war resulting from excessive or misplaced distrust. All could

benefit from a "hot line" to facilitate communication at times of crises; all could use the services of a "risk reduction center" such as was inaugurated in 1988 with respect to the risk of nuclear confrontation between the United States and the Soviet Union. However great the hostility between two camps, neither one can be well served by being drawn into war through miscalculation. Thus both India and Pakistan could have made use of an agreement to honor confidence-building measures during the crisis in January and February 1987, when each side claimed that it was massing troops at its borders in response to what the other was doing, and war became a distinct possibility.

2. *Over time, such agreements should also be extended to cover not just particular measures such as troop movements in an area but larger military policies concerning such matters as arms sales, budgeting, involvement in regional wars, and the testing, manufacture, and deployment of weapons.* Already, information concerning many such matters is openly available; much of it has become so hard to conceal that it is widely known even against the wishes of the governments most concerned. Efforts at maintaining secrecy will continue to be called for in matters clearly relevant to national security. But government officials should be required to justify publicly each policy of secrecy they take to be indispensable. As is demonstrated by the crises over secret and at times unlawful arms sales to Iran and Iraq by countries as diverse as China, Sweden, France, Israel, the Soviet Union, and the United States, such schemes often damage national security and breed more distrust domestically and abroad than any benefits associated with them could possibly warrant. Likewise, casualty figures offered by each side in conflicts such as those of Vietnam and Afghanistan are regularly at variance; again, the resulting loss of confidence outweighs any short-term gain in deceiving the domestic or international public.

3.   Confidence-building measures and policies considered in such contexts should gradually be extended to include all that is embraced in the definition of "strategy" mentioned above: not only military but also diplomatic, intelligence, commercial, cultural, and other activities that affect the level of distrust in such a way that mutual change could build confidence without impairing security. So far, the confidence-building measures adopted in the East-West arena or still at the proposal stage are of a primarily military nature. Many other practices are overdue for change; far from being confidence-building, they are confidence-destroying, and they injure participating nations as much as they damage international relations. [20] Among them are violations of law such as the mining of international waterways, the use of poison gas, and the employing, subsidizing, or training of terrorist forces. Some of the needed changes, such as those affecting intelligence-gathering and covert action, may require negotiation and mutual agreement. Just as nations bargain about arms control, so they can do much more to negotiate changes in the practices that stand in its way.

In addition, there are many circumstances in which a government takes little or no risk in giving up confidence-destroying practices unilaterally. Given the harm they do to a nation's reputation both abroad and domestically, it is important to take full advantage of such opportunities. Unilateral action is preferable whenever a nation sees a clear advantage in abandoning a harmful and counterproductive policy, such as the French policy that resulted in the Greenpeace sabotage. Likewise, policies of disinformation, once they become known, are so damaging to a nation's reputation and self-image that it is preferable to give them up immediately rather than enter into negotiation about activities so clandestine and so hard to pin down.

4.   Confidence-building measures should include, moreover, not just what is done between nations but their domestic policies insofar as they build or erode confidence. Censorship, economic exploitation, and denials of religious or political freedom not only breach fundamental moral constraints in their own right but also add considerably to the distrust a nation and its leaders inspire—abroad as well as at home. Governments that show no respect for fundamental moral constraints in their treatment of opposition forces at home inspire little confidence that they will do so abroad.

The difficulties in the way of agreements about such matters are great, since most governments reject outside interference in internal affairs, no matter how high the level of mismanagement and repression. But it is increasingly difficult to try to keep domestic and international affairs in watertight compartments.* Banking and stock market activities now cross all frontiers, so that what is done in one nation can have powerful effects across the world; the same is true of government policies that affect human rights. As a result of the reach of today's communications media, Kant's words about the world community are increasingly apt: "it has developed to the point where a violation of rights in *one* part of the world is felt *everywhere*." [21] And when, as with the human rights provisions of the Helsinki accords, human rights become matters of international agreement, then violations increase distrust still more sharply.

* It is equally unrealistic to declare them inextricably linked for purposes of negotiation. True, a government's record on human rights, its financial solvency, and its internal stability influence its reputation. But precluding talks about one area until there is progress in another is usually a recipe for inaction in both—never more dangerous than when it stands in the way of agreements to reduce the threat of war. The strategy for peace calls, rather, for patient efforts on many separate fronts, including the diplomatic one, rather than for making an effort in one area dependent on success in others.

It is important, in this respect, to take a strong stand against excessive official secrecy in all states. The policies of secrecy and censorship available to modern governments form a web that conceals many violations of moral constraints. Secrecy shields the violence, the deceit, and the betrayal that cannot tolerate the light of day. It is indispensable to the control that repressive governments exercise over their people; and it represents the greatest possible internal threat to democracies, since it renders citizens powerless to the extent that it keeps from them the information they need to influence policy.

Such official secrecy in any one state protects policies that can be directed against foreigners and fellow citizens alike, and the distrust that it engenders tempts officials in other states to work for greater secrecy as well. It is therefore the legitimate concern, not just of the citizens of the state where such secrecy prevails, but of all others to support efforts to cut it back. Guarding against the encroachments of secrecy is of fundamental importance to a strategy for peace. The task is far from hopeless, for the pervasive secrecy that many governments could exercise in the past is under attack. In the era of computers and video cassettes, officials find it increasingly difficult to keep the web of secrecy intact. And to the extent that they keep citizens from access to computers and information technology, from free travel, and from open international exchange of information, they stifle the creativity and the technological understanding needed to keep up with other nations.

5. *Finally, actions to build confidence and to undo or delay its erosion should be understood to be the business not just of governments but of public and private groups as well as individuals.* Governments are undoubtedly the most powerful agents in influencing the climate that favors or undermines

the possibility of a lasting peace. But while only they can conclude the treaties and allocate the resources that make such a peace possible, they are too often locked into long-standing modes of partisan response to conflict and are trapped in loyalties to vested interests. Without the prodding, the support, and the wealth of ideas from many quarters that a strategy for peace calls for and can draw upon, governments may never bestir themselves vigorously enough to bring about decisive change, or be able to keep up the momentum, having once begun.

Many international networks and organizations have sprung up in recent decades, and still more are needed to facilitate the implementation of a strategy for peace. The central role will nevertheless still be played by the various agencies of the United Nations. True, many member nations have used the UN for parochial purposes with no regard for the common good. But it does provide a forum for negotiation and continued debate that would be hard to replace, and its agencies carry out invaluable work in such fields as health, agriculture, literacy, refugee aid, peacekeeping, and social and cultural life. An important part of the strategy for peace must therefore be to support the UN's constructive work; to help keep its debates from derailing into partisan rhetoric and the merchandising of votes; and to stress standards for nonviolence, accuracy, and fidelity in speech no less than in action.

Just as countless industries, groups, and individuals contribute to polluting the earth's atmosphere and waters, so the climate of trust and distrust is affected by innumerable policies, large and small. Everybody, as a result, can have a part in improving that climate. Business, labor, the media, professional organizations, political parties, and religious bodies can play a leading role in this respect, both by refraining from adding to the damage through their own policies and by joining with others to bring about change. The same is true for individuals in their own lives, whether at home, at work, or in community and political activities.

While there is opportunity for all to help restore the atmosphere of minimal trust needed for human cooperation and to keep from degrading it further, the forces working in the opposite direction are formidable. Often, those who resort to deceit, violence, and lawlessness take no account of the effect of their action on the climate of trust, either in their own nation or internationally. They are strictly concerned to achieve some short-range goal or personal benefit. The same is true of industries polluting the oceans or adding to the damage from acid rain and of governments stalling joint efforts to protect the environment. They are all, in this respect, free riders when it comes to the social good at issue, willing to benefit from improvements brought about by others but unwilling to help in this regard or even to put a stop to policies adding to further deterioration.[22]

An extended scope for a strategy for peace calls for working at many levels to cut back on such policies of free riding. It matters as much to do so with respect to the social good of trust as with resources such as air or water. Such efforts, reaching beyond what is routinely thought of as related to peace, can connect a myriad of undertakings, large and small. They provide opportunities for practical steps that people can take immediately, instead of merely mouthing worn-out rhetoric about war and peace and carrying on with the symbolic gestures that have all too often seemed the only ways to express concern. All those who strive, whether individually or jointly, to reduce the sway of violence and deceit, betrayal and secrecy, are doing practical work for peace. They may be working in cities and villages torn by religious or racial conflict, or as negotiators or reporters, human rights activists, or scholars. The more they come to see that others are joined with them in such efforts, however seemingly disconnected, and the more they recognize a shared perspective and framework of fundamental constraints, the more consciously they will be part of such an expansive strategy for peace.

But the strategy is restrictive as well, in that it offers structure and guidelines. For all the many forms of action that fit in the categories I have mentioned, it is the perspective and the framework of moral constraints that structure choice. Otherwise, the risks for those working for peace are as real as for their opponents: of being co-opted into serving as mouthpieces for partisan political positions, of becoming too narrowly focused on arms policies, or of letting worthy ends justify unacceptable means. Thus, aggressive schemes to promote peace—sabotaging munitions factories, say, or spreading false rumors about militaristic government leaders—run counter to the strategy as much as do government policies of oppression at home or abroad. The same is true of disinformation and terrorism, whether undertaken by a group or a government, no matter how noble the goals they invoke to defend their actions.

A final objection arises, however, for all who wish to combine the thoroughly practical approach of Clausewitz with a strategy for peace that takes moral constraints seriously. Won't the stress on morality in international relations, no matter how understandable in principle, lead in practice either to self-righteous abuses in the name of morality or to a debilitating weakness in the face of the present crisis, instead of to the boldness it requires?

To be sure, most people would agree that this would not be so in an ideal world. But might it not be true in real life, where ignorance, partisanship, and sheer foolishness skew and corrupt all recourse to morality? Both Machiavelli and Clausewitz assert that morality does play such a counterproductive role, although they take this view to be so self-evident that they give it but the scantiest anecdotal support. The question was increasingly debated in the latter half of the nineteenth century, during decades of heightened nationalism and armaments buildup that, in turn, gave rise to a growing longing for peace, to broad peace movements, and to one peace congress after another. After the First World War—the most searing conflict the world had ever known up to that time, and one that abounded with calls for a new morality—the question of whether morality does more harm than good was raised more articulately than ever, in the name of the need for a return to realism.

CHAPTER V

Objections from a Practical Point of View

PRINCIPLES ON TRIAL

The warring state permits itself every such misdeed, every such act of violence, as would disgrace the individual man. It practices not only the accepted stratagems, but also deliberate lying and deception against the enemy; . . . [It maintains] an excess of secrecy, and a censorship of news and expressions of opinion that renders the spirits of those thus intellectually oppressed defenseless against every unfavorable turn of events and every sinister rumor. It absolves itself from the guarantees and contracts it had formed with other states, and makes unabashed confession of its rapacity and lust for power, which the private individual is then called upon to sanction in the name of patriotism.

SIGMUND FREUD, "Reflections Upon War and Death."

Freud wrote these words in 1915, shortly after the outbreak of the First World War.[1] They convey the disillusioned horror felt by so many at witnessing the brutality, the deceit, the secrecy, and the abject lawlessness of governments in wartime and, above all, at seeing their hypocrisy in prescribing standards for private individuals

that they themselves had no intention of observing. But
Freud held out little hope for change. The disillusionment,
he insisted, came from having nurtured an illusion in the
first place—the illusion that human societies had reached
a level of civilization where wars, if fought at all, would
be brief, chivalrous crusades conducted with the utmost
concern to minimize suffering and to protect noncombatants. This would never happen, he suggested, since the
most primitive instincts lie close to the surface in all societies. The layer of socially imposed moral constraints is
vanishingly thin, easily damaged in times of conflict. Wars
would continue to be as bitter and cruel as ever, only more
and more destructive because of the growing "perfection"
of weapons. Freud ended, in utter pessimism, by suggest-
ing that the saying "If you desire peace, prepare for war"
might now best be paraphrased as "If you would endure
life, be prepared for death."²

Across the Atlantic, President Woodrow Wilson expressed similar horror over the conduct of the Great War.
But he drew exactly the opposite conclusions. For him,
the illusion lay in taking that conduct to reflect a permanent fact of human nature and thus giving up the effort to
seek a moral world order. The standard of government
conduct should be set as high as that of personal conduct,
and nothing should be allowed to stand in the way of
enforcing it. The majority of the world's citizens loathed
war and violence, secrecy, and oppression; if only their
voices could be heard, he argued, and if only leaders were
to seek "open convenants openly arrived at," reform
would be irresistible.

As the United States prepared to enter the war, hopes
rose that the resulting infusion of force and idealism could
indeed bring an end to all future wars. Wilson's stature, at
home and abroad, lent credence to these hopes. Here was
a man with the broad and generous perspective and the
moral principles that Kant had called for. Having been

granted unprecedented power to put them into practice, he had formulated a strategy informed both by scholarship and practical politics. Above all, he had the will to give himself wholeheartedly to this task.

Wilson was convinced, moreover, that it was America's task to show the way. He insisted that the principles of America were also those of mankind. America's flag, he claimed, was humanity's flag; and there could be no retreat, no compromising the cause of that humanity. Before him, many had spoken of the "white man's burden" in civilizing the world; in 1891, W. T. Stead had written that "the English-speaking race is one of the chief of God's chosen agents for executing coming improvements in the lot of mankind." [3] That Wilson had narrowed the leadership role to his country alone surprised few who had witnessed the nation's euphoria over "manifest destiny" in previous decades.

By the beginning of the Paris Peace Conference in 1919, Wilson's fervor was such that a tight-lipped Georges Clemenceau likened him to Moses bearing the Ten Commandments. Inexperienced in foreign affairs, he was unprepared for the maelstrom of forces confronting him. His strategy of persuasion had been formulated without adequate attention to the "friction" of which Clausewitz had written. Before long, increasingly ill and fatigued, Wilson had seen most of his Fourteen Points cut back. The secret deliberations and machinations at the conference made his "open covenants openly arrived at" a meaningless phrase. Conquered populations, far from being free to choose their nationality, were ruthlessly divided up to satisfy European powers. French and British demands for exorbitant German reparations carried the day. And in the end, Wilson's fellow Americans rejected the League of Nations, which he had worked so hard to establish.

It was inevitable that Wilson's missionary zeal and the collapse of his efforts would trouble even those who were

in sympathy with many of his internationalist goals. His
moralistic stance and his failure to take the realities of
practical politics into consideration made many observers
recoil, not only from his advocacy of a new moral order,
but from taking morality into account at all in the conduct
of foreign policy. Their views were reinforced as they
heard endless bombast about peace in the decades after the
War and winced at lofty but impotent proposals such as
the 1928 Kellogg-Briand Pact outlawing war.

Seasoned observers like Hans Morgenthau, Raymond
Aron, and George Kennan reacted against such impractical
idealism by adopting what they called a "realist" stance in
international politics.[4] Their attitude, close to that of Clausewitz but more carefully worked out, was one of strong
opposition to what they saw as a moralistic approach to
foreign policy. The first business of government, they argued, is not what is right in some abstract sense but what
best serves a nation's interest. To act otherwise is likely to
encourage false expectations and to bring about political
failures resulting in needless human suffering. Thus Morgenthau held that the First World War had been prolonged
unnecessarily beyond merely securing the defeat of the
enemy in order to "make the world safe for democracy."
Those who insisted on morality in foreign policy have
been, according to such realist views, innocuous utopians
and hypocrites at best and, at worst, fanatics willing to go
to any length to impose their views.

Underlying the realist conclusion that it is impossible
to rely on morality in foreign policy, one often finds a
relativist claim: if we look at the many conflicting moral
principles that have been invoked by governments
through the centuries, we shall be hard put to find any
unanimity. Apart from windy generalizations, no moral
values hold for all societies. Thus, George Kennan notes
in a recent article that "there are no internationally accepted standards of morality to which the U.S. govern-

ment could appeal if it wished to act in the name of moral principles."⁵

Up to a point, Kennan is surely right. It is true that standards differ from nation to nation and that even the most widely known moral codes, such as the Ten Commandments or the Buddhist Five Precepts, overlap only in part. This should caution reformers against imagining that others must adopt, wholesale, the particular ideals common in their own societies. But it does not prove Kennan's claim that there are *no* internationally recognized moral standards; for, as suggested in Chapter II, the codes do have much in common concerning the most fundamental constraints—on violence, deceit, and betrayal in particular—that human societies have sought to impose on conduct. Breaking a truce was as reprehensible in Homer's day as it is in our time. And the practices of genocide and other atrocities in our century have received near-universal condemnation.

There is nothing mysterious or self-contradictory about showing what the American Declaration of Independence called "a decent respect to the opinions of mankind." The fact that not all cultures have identical moral standards should not lead us to conclude that they can agree on none. Nor is everything lost just because there is disagreement on the moral judgments we take to be fundamental. Fanatics may argue that genocide is morally legitimate; this does nothing to undermine the authority of the general consensus on the issue.

Even if realists were to find such an argument persuasive in principle, it would do nothing to alter their condemnation of those who invoke morality in international affairs, for their central point is an utterly practical one. What does it matter if the governments of, say, Chile, South Africa, Afghanistan, or Iran solemnly join in condemning torture, so long as they continue to practice it? Hypocrisy and inconsistency have been the rule in foreign policy, not the exception, as debates in the U.N. General Assembly can make painfully clear. The governments most zealous in pointing to the vices of others tend to think nothing of their own, while accepting those of their allies without batting an eyelash. Leaders have too often invoked morality to cover up for particularly egregious actions. Throughout history, the cruelest crusades and most vicious inquisitions have been conducted in the name of some religious or secular dogma that was declared so exalted, so self-evidently superior as to justify any amount of violence and persecution.

It was against such a background that George Kennan warned against "the carrying over into the affairs of states of the concepts of right and wrong, the assumption that state behavior is a fit subject for moral judgment." Such assumptions, though rooted in a desire to do away with war and violence,

> make violence more enduring, more terrible, and more destructive to political stability than did the older motives of national interest. A war fought in the name of high moral principle finds no early end short of some form of total domination.[6]

Public officials responsible for blatantly aggressive policies often invoke moral principles quite cynically, without taking them seriously for one moment. But if aggressors believe in the righteousness of their cause, they are—if anything—even more dangerous. To the extent that they identify their own cause with all that is good, and their adversary with Satan or absolute evil, they are especially likely to fall prey to the pathology of partisanship: their perspective may contract to the point where they no longer stop to question actions that they would otherwise find repugnant. In either case, whether they use moral language cynically or self-righteously, the discrepancy between their words and their actions generates distrust both at home and abroad.

The fact that governments have so often invoked moral principles naively, hypocritically, inconsistently, or in order to exploit and oppress, justifies every caution. Moralistic language can indeed be counterproductive. But this conclusion hardly proves that all moral principles should be set aside in practical contexts. Causing harm poses a greater problem for someone concerned to act morally than for one who has jettisoned all such concern. It is self-contradictory to insist on abandoning all moral concerns in international relations on the (inherently moral) grounds of wanting to reduce suffering. To do so is also unnecessary. Laws and medicine can also be abused, yet no one suggests that they should be abolished. It is hypocrisy and abuse that should be fought, not the laws or the medicine or the moral principles themselves.

This distinction finds illustration in Woodrow Wilson's own presidency. In spite of his railing against U.S. intervention in Central America, more such interventions took place during his term of office than during any previous period. His explanations were of the most idealistic nature: thus, after the bombardment of Vera Cruz in April 1914, he assured the world that the United States had "gone down to Mexico to serve mankind."[7] At the very least, such claims raise doubts about Wilson's sincerity and about his consistency in invoking his ideal of nonintervention. But our legitimate doubts about Wilson do nothing either to support or to undercut the principle of nonintervention itself. Similarly, the fact that South African officials discourse on the need for nonviolence, while engaging in ruthless violence against blacks and dissenters and against neighboring nations, shows blatant hypocrisy and inconsistency; but it does nothing to prove that *all* appeals for nonviolence are worthless and insincere.

Wilson's realist critics were surely right in showing how such dissonance between language and action serves only to increase public skepticism and distrust. But it was an illusion for them to suppose that a sphere of foreign affairs could be separated out from domestic affairs and denuded of moral considerations. It was an illusion, too, and one increasingly anachronistic in the nuclear era, to believe that if every nation tried to steer clear of moral language, common survival would somehow be better ensured through the workings of some unseen hand or of a balance of power. Realism today requires the abandonment of these illusions, but it also calls for heeding the warnings of Morgenthau and Kennan and others against moralizing and the abuses that it has so often brought in its wake. If, as I have argued, moral constraints are now indispensable in international relations as elsewhere, but if they are also, as the realists suggest, likely to be misused out of hypocrisy, ignorance, or fanaticism, then it matters to recognize what forms this misuse takes and to minimize each one.

MORALIZERS

Hang up my hairshirt, put my scourge in place,
and pray, Laurent, for Heaven's perpetual grace.
I'm going to the prison now, to share
my last few coins with the wretches there.

MOLIERE, *Tartuffe*

Spotting moralizers and attempting to puncture their inflated claims is not only pleasurable but also essential, lest they go unchallenged and inflict the harm of which realists rightly warn. To call people moralizers is to reject the surface meaning of what they say and to point to the incongruity between their high-flown talk and their squalid, insensitive, often brutal behavior.★

Among moralizers, hypocrites make the easiest targets, with their pompous intoning of moral standards that they are the first to break. In his portrait of Tartuffe, Molière depicts such a figure to perfection, one who speaks of very little except morality while scheming to defraud his unsuspecting host and to seduce his wife. Every age has its own archetypal hypocrites, yet they call forth the same responses. The falsehearted kiss of a Judas, the pious fraud of venal TV evangelists, the thundering rejection of drug trafficking or deals with terrorists by those who support such practices in secret—once the discrepancy between word and deed becomes known, derision and distrust are utterly reasonable responses.

A second type of moralizer is the individual who is high-handed in the face of human complexity—someone who brings simplistic remedies to bear where they have no place. Such people distort reality, either to make their simple precepts fit or to convince themselves that even

---

★ The noun "moralizer" and the verb "to moralize" have only recently acquired this negative meaning. (The same is true to a lesser but still significant extent of "moralist.") In earlier centuries, "moralize" had one of two other meanings, both descriptive rather than critical. In the first sense, "moralize" simply meant to interpret something morally or to make something the subject of moral reflection—the activity of anyone who speaks or writes about moral issues. Second, "moralize" was used in the sense of speaking didactically, so as to improve the morals of others. But again, this meaning was descriptive, rather than signaling something inherently problematic. After all, was not such improvement the avowed purpose of moral and religious discourse? Fables ended in a "moral"; so did many cautionary tales. It has taken the growing questioning of such activities to help shift the meaning of the word "moralize" to a third sense: that of using moral language inappropriately, manipulatively, often exploitatively.

their most dubious actions have solid moral foundations. In this category fall priests who, in their zeal to condemn contraception, wax lyrical about the joys of motherhood to women watching their children starve. So do isolationists who still believe it possible to protect their nation from foreign wars, drugs, and epidemics simply by sealing off its borders; as well as those who hope that some mass transformation of human consciousness will eliminate war. Woodrow Wilson's critics thought that he was a moralizer in both senses of the word: he did not live up to the standards that he proclaimed to others, and he appeared to apply overly simple homilies to a world situation requiring far subtler understanding.

Yet a third type of moralizing overlaps with the second. Those who fall in this category seem excessively strict and uncompromising, given the circumstances, and too eager to punish the slightest infraction of a rule as a severe moral crime. In this category, too, fall those who do not appear to realize when moral discourse is out of place—who sermonize to children too young to understand what is at issue, or who intrude their judgment where they have no right to do so. Parents, teachers, and judges have to guard against such tendencies; the activities of censors and book burners of every era show how dangerous it is to succumb to moralizing of this kind. Aristotle points out that is far from easy to do or say what one thinks is called for "to the right person, in the right amount, at the right time, for the right end, and in the right way, . . . nor can everyone do it."[8] Those who are clumsiest—at times blindest—in misjudging to whom, when, and how to bring up moral issues are all moralizers of this type.

A fourth type of moralizer, finally, and often the most dangerous, is so obsessed by the desire to combat what he or she takes to be some particular evil as to ride

roughshod over other moral principles. The stalker of sexual transgressions who tramples all respect for privacy, the
Spanish Inquisitors or Chinese Red Guards willing to be-
tray, torture, and kill in order to eradicate what they saw
as doctrinal deviance, and zealots of every kind fall into
this category. Fanaticism, as Jeremy Bentham points out,
"never sleeps, is never glutted . . . it is never stopped by
conscience for it has pressed conscience into its service."[9]
The four types of moralizing sometimes overlap. In
each, what is said or done is at odds with what the situation calls for. Moralizers do not seem to perceive themselves, or those to whom or about whom they are
speaking, in anything like a realistic way; and since their
perception is inadequate, their response is bound to be
flawed. Their appeals to morality, as a result, seem to spin
in the void, except for those unfortunate enough to be
their victims.

Humor and, above all, satire is the quintessential
means for stripping away the pretense of such talk, exposing it as what La Rochefoucauld called "the homage that
vice pays to virtue."[10] Such irreverence is indispensable
for learning to understand oneself and others; for achieving the humility without which, as La Rochefoucauld also
wrote, "we perpetuate all our vices"; and for coming to
know in whom one can and cannot place trust.[11]

When such perspective is lacking, efforts to guard
against moralizing merely provide a ready-made excuse
for rejecting all criticism of one's conduct. It is commonplace for those on one side of a dispute to deride those on
the other as hypocritical, unseeing, and overzealous con-
veyors of simplistic homilies, while characterizing themselves as realistic. As Bertrand Russell said, "A Realist is a
man who confirms the prejudices of the man who is
speaking."[12] The Nazis were masters at thus dismissing
their critics as moralizers. Hans Fritzsche, for example, a

prominent propagandist for Nazi Germany during the Second World War, regularly castigated the British on these grounds during his radio broadcasts. England, he said, could be likened to a "moralizing tea-drinking governess who faints if anyone treads on the tail of her lapdog."[13]

Singling out one's opponents as moralizers and stressing the realism of one's own views can therefore itself be far too simplistic. Like moralizing in its own right, it, too, can represent a distortion of perception—a failure fully to see oneself and those to whom or about whom one speaks, so as not to have to feel, imagine, or think about what might be at issue. The more rigid one's beliefs, the greater one's temptation to see all who dare to criticize them as not only wrong but knowingly, hypocritically wrong. And if these others seem to embrace their error sincerely, then the temptation is strong to dismiss them as self-deceived—another epithet too easily flung at opponents.

This attitude is common among those whose religious or political commitments are so strong that they take all who disagree with them to be deluded. It can also afflict persons so immersed in practical affairs, and so certain of the wise judgment that long experience has honed in them, that they begin to discount opposing views too quickly. It then represents the collapse, on the plane of debate, of the broad and informed perspective that many realist critics of moralizing have rightly stressed.[14] It turns into yet another form of partisanship. Just as the adoption of a relentlessly moralistic tone can prevent leaders from seeing a conflict from different points of view and responding to it appropriately, so the corresponding zeal against their moralizing can have the same effect.

Instead of merely dismissing those who disagree with them as moralizers, public officials need to consider the evidence for judging someone hypocritical, simplistic, uncompromising, or perhaps fanatical. To steer clear of such attitudes, they might try to avoid breaching in practice the principles that they proclaim, lest they be thought hypocrites; to reach for an expanded perspective and sober practical judgment in order not to appear simplistic; to entertain the possibility of exceptions rather than open themselves to the charge of undue severity; and to accept the whole framework of four constraints rather than just one or two, so as to avoid the risk of excessive zeal or fanaticism.

For a view of the combination of sensitivity and practical diplomatic experience that avoids either moralizing or judging all one's critics to be moralizers, it is worth turning to a work by the British diplomat and author Harold Nicolson. In *Peacemaking, 1919,* he looks back at having gone to the Paris Conference as a young man burning with idealism, eager to be of help, however minimal, in curing the ills brought on by war.[15] He describes his growing awareness of the difficulties that stood in the way of achieving a lasting peace. Some were in his view altogether inevitable, such as the emotions, so soon after the war, of the public and the press in each of the participating countries; others seemed to him unavoidable given the failure of vision and sense of direction of the world's leaders at the time; still others, such as the flaws and imprecisions in the armistice agreement, the delay in beginning the talks, and the confusion attending the debates, could in his view have been averted with a little forethought. If there is to be a lasting peace, those who prepare for it will need to achieve a perspective endowed with the vision, direction, and foresight that Nicolson found so deplorably absent at the conference.

But more than perspective was at issue at the conference as described by Nicolson. Seeing President Wilson's passionate advocacy of certain moral principles as necessary to the peace process, he shows how the president's increasing physical and mental disability and his tragic errors at the negotiations contributed to the betrayal of his ideals. And yet Nicolson held fast to what he considered the fundamental core of rightness in Wilson's ideals, and so could not go along with the simplistic forms of condemnation that were so tempting at the time and for decades afterwards. Looking back in 1933 at Wilson's advocacy of fundamental moral principles, Nicolson writes:

> In the main tenets of his political philosophy I believed with fervent credulity. In spite of bitter disillusionment I believe in them today. I believed, with him, that the standard of political and international conduct should be as high, as sensitive, as the standard of personal conduct. I believed, and I still believe, that the only true patriotism is an active desire that one's own tribe or country should in every particular minister to that ideal. I shared with him a hatred of violence in any form, and a loathing of despotism in any form. I conceived, as he conceived, that this hatred was common to the great mass of humanity . . .[16]

Nicolson wrote his book in part to offer advice for later efforts at peacemaking and governing more generally. He showed how public officials can be alert to the risks of moralizing that Wilson exemplified without falling prey to the disillusioned rejection of all moral guidelines. Only by adopting a perspective that helps them to guard against a partial and skewed understanding of the situation before them can they have a chance to think it through and negotiate about it with the care it deserves.

Even if government officials achieve such a perspec-

tive, however, another difficulty confronts them: how
should they respond to a situation in which they find
themselves forced to choose between two evils? A situation, for instance, in which they have to break one promise in order to honor another, or expose innocent people
to the risk of death in order to minimize the risk of a
massacre? I considered such dilemmas in Chapter IV. The
practical conflicts that they raise for public servants have
long been discussed under the heading of "dirty hands."

DIRTY HANDS AND PRACTICAL POLITICS

Claims that one must at times dirty one's hands to serve
the public interest differ from "might makes right" arguments in that they recognize the force of moral constraints. They take their departure from the necessity that
most people acknowledge for occasional exceptions to
such constraints in practical dilemmas. In order to serve
one's community or one's nation, according to such
claims, one may have to act against a strong moral conviction when the only choice is between two evils, and
accept the sense of guilt—sometimes the punishment—
that ensues.

Few would dispute that such choices arise. Officials
entrusted with the responsibility for a community's welfare may find it harder than private individuals to escape
them altogether. A second claim, however, goes beyond
stressing the anguish of being forced to make choices of
that nature. It holds that even the most principled and
public-spirited leaders must expect to get their hands dirty
if they want to get anything done. They must therefore
prepare themselves by learning, as Machiavelli insisted,
how *not* to be good. The mark of their integrity, according
to such a view, is that they experience compunction; the

mark of their good sense, that they overcome it when their goals so require.[17]

Michael Walzer writes about a harsh dilemma of this nature for a newly elected official: although opposed to torture, he gives the order to inflict it on "a captured rebel leader who knows or probably knows the location of a number of bombs hidden in apartment buildings around the city, set to go off within the next few hours."[18] His willingness to acknowledge and bear his guilt is evidence, Walzer argues, "both that he is not too good for politics and that he is good enough. Here is the moral politician; it is by his dirty hands that we know him."

Perhaps the best-known discussion of the choices thus posed for those who want to serve the public interest was set forth by Max Weber in 1918.[19] Having known at close hand the horrors of the First World War, and nearing the end of his life, Weber had a far darker outlook on politics than that of Woodrow Wilson. The tasks of politics, Weber argued, can be accomplished only by means of violence. Deceit and breaches of faith are part of the game as well. They must be used with good judgment and a sense of responsibility; but those who refuse all such methods invite failure and defeat, perhaps at the hands of entirely unscrupulous leaders. Worst of all, in their absolutist strivings for ultimate ends, such innocents turn too easily to the most brutal stratagems. Religious or revolutionary "warriors of faith," Weber held, may then urge their followers to use force just one last time so as to bring about a situation "in which all violence is annihilated."[20]

Weber's article is still required reading in courses on government today. It is a powerful effort to dispel simplistic postwar optimism and to combat the facile justification of barbarism in the name of the highest ideals. All who enter politics can feel the tension that Weber describes between wanting to do what they consider right, come what may, and having to compromise out of concern for the consequences of their actions. Many have witnessed, in themselves or in their colleagues, how corrupting either alternative can become in practice.

But Weber, after making these points with passion and subtlety, has no advice for those who might wish to avoid either form of corruption. He offers no support for his bitter assumption that all who engage in politics must open themselves to diabolic forces.[21] Nor does he distinguish, in this respect, between the experience of different leaders and of nations at different periods in their history. He overlooks the dangerous seductiveness of seeing onself as a tragic hero, forced to do the unspeakable for the sake of the community's greater good. And the stark dichotomy that he sets up between what he calls the ethic of ultimate ends and that of responsibility leaves to one side a large part of the subtle process of moral deliberation about principles and practical cases that politics at its best requires.[22]

Without such deliberation, most people not unexpectedly opt too soon for compromising their principles. Just as unreflective appeals to morality too often turn, in practice, into moralizing, so unreflecting appeals to the "dirty hands" rationale too often turn, in practice, into needless and unjustified exceptions to moral principles. It is not surprising, therefore, though it would surely trouble Weber and most thinkers who have written on the subject, that in practical politics the expression "dirty hands" has turned into a code word among public servants —one brought in to accommodate a multitude of "dirty tricks." Those who invoke the rationale of dirty hands so liberally may be paying lip service to morality; but they ignore the constraints it calls for and have jettisoned its requirements for careful deliberation about how the constraints apply to their own situation. Gone are the scruples and the personal anguish of which Weber wrote; gone his awareness of the risks of corruption. Often, all that remains is a quick calculation of pros and cons that includes a side mention of the guilt attached to dirty hands.[23]

Dirty-hands calculations come most easily when the intended victims are foreign. Bias and partisanship lead some to assume that the lives of foreigners count less than those of fellow citizens; and fear of exposure and of legal repercussions adds to the incentives for exercising more restraint at home than abroad. As a result, dirty-hands excuses are often brought in to buttress practices such as psychological warfare, disinformation, counterinsurgency, covert operations, and destabilization. To keep these activities from public awareness, officials may engage in deceit, shredding documents, establishing false chronologies—and the cover-ups, once again, are justified on similar grounds. Governments now pursue these ancient policies of aggression and deceit on a global scale with the aid of the most up-to-date technology. Private groups using similar methods likewise take for granted that they must dirty their own hands if they want to serve their political or social ideals.*

The problem with allowing such casual and wide leeway for exceptions to moral constraints is that it opens the

---

* In his Postscript (p. 155), Erik Erikson points to psychoanalytical associations to the expression "dirty hands." The proverbial saying "He that toucheth pitch shall be defiled therewith" (Ecclesiasticus 13:1) recalls the indelible nature of the guilt associated with certain moral violations. The common use of the expression "dirty hands" may also relate to a different meaning, in which people are criticized for refusing to take part in work of a physically messy nature, such as cooking or child care, or farming, expecting others to carry out all such tasks. Finally, the expression, when invoked as an excuse in politics, may be meant to suggest that those who lie or kill for the public good soil only what is peripheral—their hands—rather than compromising their spirit or integrity.[24]

door, in practice, to abuses as great as those made possible by a simplistically applied absolutist approach. Here, as with moralizing, it would help public officials to consider all the ways in which such abuses take root and grow. This would alert them to the need not just to consider the short-range goal they might wish to achieve through, for example, a disinformation campaign regarding an adversary, but also to be aware of all the ways in which such a practice invites imitation and retaliation. They would then perceive the difficulty of resisting the temptation to engage in further violations of moral standards, having once chosen that path, and would note the corresponding ease with which hypocrisy can serve to explain expedient breaches of the very principles one propounds.

The common failure to reflect on moral aspects of situations is reinforced by likening all choices to extreme cases where nothing but violent or deceitful or treacherous tactics seems capable of averting a great catastrophe—say, lying to confuse a terrorist threatening to blow up an entire city. It is then easy to conclude that most ordinary moral difficulties also call for compromise. But daily political choices are rarely of such an excruciating nature. Quick cost-benefit calculations, even if they take into account the agent's experience of dirty hands, often ignore the long-term costs—including the costs to the integrity and the reputation of agents, to others affected by their actions, and to the climate of distrust—of ignoring or breaching fundamental moral constraints.[25] Above all, such calculations fail to take into account the *cumulative* impact on that climate from the policies of violence and deceit, betrayal and secrecy that they help perpetuate.[26] Within the confines of such a cramped perspective, strategy loses all foresight and moral language is reduced to empty moralizing.

Once these considerations are brought into the debate, those who wish to embark on actions that violate what they know are fundamental moral standards would have to accept a heavy burden of justification, rather than rest satisfied with the casual short-term calculation that is too often the rule. A careful process of considering the justification of difficult choices is utterly different from the Machiavellian advice to "learn how not to be good." If taken seriously, such a process would help agents make sure that there is no way of escaping the choice between the two evils, perhaps through some alternative way of acting. Doing so would eliminate the vast majority of actions now undertaken in the name of the necessity for public officials to dirty their hands. In the remaining cases, where no such alternatives exist, the process could help officials ascertain which is in fact the lesser, rather than the greater, of the two evils.

One reason that overly hasty forms of both moralizing and dirty-hands reasoning fail to respond to the circumstances of difficult cases is that they skip past all such steps of deliberation to arrive at a conclusion. In that way, they facilitate biased perception and stunted deliberation. Just as we have to counter the practical damage of moralizing, so we have to insist, in order to cope with the practical damage of opportunistic dirty-hands reasoning, that those exceptions be rare and that they carry a heavy burden of proof. It is unreasonable to imagine that no further standards of judgment apply once one allows for exceptions.

What is needed, rather, is careful attention to the criteria by which such exceptions might be singled out, a firm grasp of the framework of moral constraints, and clear procedures for accountability to justify actions taken and to prevent abuses from arising and spreading. When it comes to public officials in a democracy choosing whether or not to engage in "dirty tricks," the test of publicity discussed in Chapters II and IV requires full accountability to the public or to its elected representatives. Otherwise, the appeal to dirty hands will continue to serve as the loose omnibus rationalization that it has become for many public officials intent on casting aside inconvenient moral constraints.

At this point, however, yet another objection is raised to the claim that such constraints have a place in the practice of international relations. Government leaders or policy analysts might agree with my argument that these constraints need not deteriorate into moralizing or be nullified by overly hasty dirty-hands reasoning. They might acknowledge the benefits of the changes that a strategy for peace calls for, and be clear about the risk to their nation and to humanity of failing to bring them about. Yet, some among them might still hold back. Given today's insecure circumstances, these advocates of a no-holds-barred foreign policy could argue, it would be foolhardy to abandon long-standing practices on moral grounds. Rather, all means—no matter how disreputable—must be at the disposal of their government for reasons of strict self-defense. In times of great danger, national self-interest must outweigh all other considerations.

THE IMPERATIVE OF SELF-DEFENSE

We can assume *nothing* where the Communist leaders are concerned. We can trust *nothing* that the Communist leaders say. We can accept *nothing* that the Communist leaders sign as a conclusive guarantee.
BARRY GOLDWATER, *Why Not Victory?*

Granted, a strategist of the old school may argue: some of our international practices are unsavory and go

against our fundamental values. Granted, too, these practices often injure us as much as others and reduce the
chances for collective action to overcome the threat of
nuclear annihilation. But let's be realistic. Barry Goldwater is right: trust is a luxury we cannot afford.

Besides, what alternatives do we possess, this strategist might continue, to the policies we now reluctantly
endorse? Kant uttered his strictures in a less desperate period; now we are dealing with adversaries who can wipe
us out at a moment's notice. Because they threaten our
survival, we have to be able to disregard even fundamental
rules in sheer self-defense. We would be only too glad to
play by those rules if we could trust others to do the same.
But the world has become too dangerous for us to abide
by principles that our adversaries violate at will. We cannot disarm unilaterally when it comes to bribery, disinformation, or violent destabilization of third-world nations,
any more than with respect to military defense.

In many nations at war or threatened by war, strategists of this persuasion can be heard making the same
argument: "Dishonorable stratagems," to use Kant's
phrase, may indeed erode trust, undermine negotiations,
and thus increase the risk to national as well as joint survival in the long run. But a nation will put its values and
its safety even more directly at risk if it lowers its guard
out of misguided concern with moral niceties.

Few would quarrel with the need to be on guard in a
world as dangerous as ours. Nations need to exercise
every ounce of distrust that promotes their freedom and
survival. It is certainly important, moreover, for a government not to let the attacks or dirty tricks of adversaries
go unanswered, nor to be victimized by passively accepting such policies.

Yet the need for extreme caution and for responding
to an adversary's unacceptable conduct does not by itself

justify repaying injuries in the same coin. Two wrongs do not make a right in foreign policy any more than elsewhere. Forceful responses can take many lawful forms, such as the use of sanctions, diplomatic protests, and multilateral action.[27] And though retaliation in kind against treachery and violence may have its emotional appeal—the more so since those who violate the rights of others invite disrespect for their own rights—it tends to corrupt participants, heighten mutual partisanship, hurt innocent bystanders, and impel those at the receiving end to strike back still more vengefully. The predicament of Lebanon shows how such mutual retaliation in kind can escalate. As one observer wrote of the unrestrained factional conflicts there since 1975, "Beirut became synonymous with a new barbarity, its very name becoming shorthand in the world's headlines for chaos, as the Congo had two decades earlier."[28]

Old-school strategists might well agree that governments should not indulge in retaliation in kind so long as lawful alternatives will check aggression on the part of an adversary.* It is only when the liberty or the survival of a nation is at stake that they take all means to be fair. Thus Machiavelli holds, in the *Discourses,* that there should be no talk of justice or injustice, humanity or cruelty, honor or dishonor, where "the safety of one's country" is at stake.[29] And in 1954, a commission chaired by former

---

* Around 1750 B.C., when the Code of Hammurabi first spoke of exacting an eye from a noble who had put out the eye of another noble, and the teeth from one who had knocked out another's teeth, retaliation in kind represented an advance over blood feuds, and massive retaliation. Justice called for equivalence of retribution, not excess, and was to be carried out according to the code by lawful authorities, not by an aggrieved party with a mind to revenge. The same was true when "an eye for an eye, a tooth for a tooth, a hand for a hand, a foot for a foot" was prescribed for the Jews in the Book of Exodus.

President Herbert Hoover restated such a view in cold war terms:

> It is now clear that we are facing an implacable enemy whose avowed objective is world domination by whatever means and at whatever cost. There are no rules in such a game. Hitherto acceptable norms of human conduct do not apply. If the U.S. is to survive, long-standing American concepts of "fair play" must be reconsidered. . . . We must learn to subvert, sabotage and destroy our enemies by more clever, more sophisticated and more effective methods than those used against us. . .[30]

The view that there are no rules for what a nation can do when thus threatened represents an unwarranted stretching of a claim that most people would accept: that ordinary moral constraints should allow for limited exceptions as a last resort when self-defense is at issue. Such a claim is based on a nearly universal view that staying alive is the most basic human imperative, shared with all living beings. But strategists who want their governments to be free to violate moral constraints at will in foreign affairs stretch this claim in two ways. They extend the reach both of what counts as self-defense and of the exceptions it allows. It is worth considering each of these two extensions, since they provide the basis for rejecting moral concerns about foreign policy in times of prolonged national emergency.

The force of self-defense as a justification for going to war rests on a long-standing analogy between nations defending themselves and individuals doing so—by means of violence as a last resort, if need be. Such a response to aggression has seemed self-evidently right to all but those pacifists who accept no grounds for resorting to violence.

Erasmus, Kant, and other advocates of projects for a lasting peace were once among the few who held self-defense to be the *only* legitimate reason for a nation's engaging in war.[31] Others saw as justified, in addition, certain wars of punishment, retaliation, or religious or political conquest. But even they took for granted that self-defense offered the strongest grounds for resorting to violence. By now, the levels of suffering and injustice inflicted by wars of conquest have given pause to those who hold expansive views of what makes for a righteous war. As a result, there is now greater agreement in law, theology, and philosophy alike, that only self-defense (including aiding in the defense of allies and victimized peoples) can offer sufficient justification for war.[32]

For an example of a conflict in which such a reason was clearly present on one side and absent on the other, consider the Nazi attack on the Spanish town of Guernica on April 26, 1937. Hitler had sent the Luftwaffe to bomb the town as a gesture of support for General Franco's Fascist forces. When the planes arrived, the town market was thronging with villagers who had come to sell their produce. Incendiary bombs exploded everywhere, destroying the town and killing over fifteen hundred men, women, and children. In such an emergency, most would agree that the citizens of Guernica would have had every right to defend themselves against the Nazi assault, had they had the means to do so. The Germans, on the other hand, could hardly claim self-defense in justification of their action. Hitler and Franco chose, instead, to have their supporters spread the propaganda message that "Red hordes" had carried out the massacre.

Half a century after the Nazi assault on Guernica, death brought suddenly to civilians from the air is no longer unusual. Even after the Second World War, with its millions of civilian casualties, napalm and firebombs have rained on villagers in Vietnam, Afghanistan, and elsewhere. But by now, those who order or carry out such assaults rarely hesitate to claim that their actions are justified by the imperative of self-defense—of their nation, their allies, their way of life, their religious or political convictions. Just as rulers on opposite sides of past wars once took for granted that God was on their side, so opponents now invoke self-defense and national security even for aggressive ventures far beyond their borders.

Such actions are far from analogous to what an individual might rightfully do as a last resort when faced with direct assault. But because of the ferocity of today's weapons and the genuine threat to national survival, the great powers as well as adversaries in regional conflicts can now argue, as they never could before, that everything they do to reinforce their own power and that of their allies, or to diminish that of their enemies, actually does contribute to self-defense. Thus some U.S. policymakers argue that they must respond in kind to the disinformation, bribery, violent destabilization of foreign governments, and other tactics employed by the Soviet Union across the world or risk losing influence in one region after another. Others likewise invoke the legitimacy of such self-protection not only for what they do in wartime, or only for their military preparations in peacetime, but for all economic, political, and other policies that affect their nation's international standing. Self-defense, when seen in such a light, becomes coextensive with all of strategy.

Up to a point, it is reasonable and indeed indispensable for present-day governments to go beyond the individual analogy in deciding what their nation's security requires. Given the nature of contemporary weapons systems, it would be absurd to prepare defenses merely against direct attacks; for by the time such attacks occur, it is often too late for genuine self-protection. And yet it

is clearly excessive to move to the other extreme of justifying all questionable activities that have an effect, however tenuous or remote, on national defense. It remains
necessary to draw a line as close as possible to the analogy
with what individuals might do to defend themselves—a
line that distinguishes between legitimate self-defense and
all that a nation might do to expand its territory and further its ideological aims.

It is useful, for the purpose of drawing such a line, to
consider the distinction often made between the narrower
concept of self-defense and the larger one of self-preservation.[33] Acts of self-defense presuppose a specific threat
of serious injury from particular agents; self-preservation
include such acts along with all that makes for greater
safety and well-being. Preventive health care, for instance,
can add to longevity and well-being and, in that sense, to
self-preservation, without counting as self-defense in the
same way as shielding oneself against blows. It is especially with respect to self-defense properly speaking that
one may ask about limited exceptions to fundamental
moral constraints such as that on violence. When it comes
to the larger aims of self-preservation, the analogy between individual and state action holds: it is no more legitimate for a landowner to bribe, cheat, or terrorize
unscrupulous neighbors than for a state to do so, no matter how much those responsible might claim to be better
off and safer as a result.

The distinction between the narrower concept of self-
defense and the larger one of self-preservation is clear in
the case of policies of terrorism and disinformation. Terrorism cannot be defended on grounds of direct self-
defense, because its random assaults on noncombatants
hardly disarm assailants. Disinformation programs, because they are so diffuse and so likely to boomerang, are
equally worthless from the point of view of direct self-
defense. Nor can advocates of these two practices claim to

be engaging in them for the purpose of giving humanitarian aid to beleaguered peoples—least of all terrorists, whose actions represent a denial of the most fundamental human rights.

The confusion that results from ignoring the distinction between the narrower and larger concepts is increased by a second way of stretching the claim regarding self-defense. When government officials state, as in the Hoover commission report mentioned above, that "there are no rules" where national security is at issue, they may not intend to be taken literally. But such statements open the door to every form of abuse; for they can be used to nullify the efforts over many centuries to draw distinctions between legitimate and illegitimate means of warfare. International law, just war theory, and military education all specify certain rules—against killing noncombatants, say, or torturing prisoners or using poison gas. True, the rules are often overridden in practice; but those who become convinced that no rules apply to what they do risk losing all moral inhibitions in this respect.

Together, the two efforts to stretch the justification for what can be done in self-defense undermine constraints with respect to foreign policy in times of peace as of war. They then introduce yet another way to reject moral concerns in foreign affairs. The claim is no longer that of realists in earlier decades, that international relations are somehow inherently outside the bounds of morality. It is, rather, that the appeal to self-defense legitimates all actions pertaining to foreign policy, once they are understood to be inseparable from a nation's or a community's survival, and that they are therefore governed by no rules.

The risk of nuclear war doubtless helps make this claim more acceptable to policymakers; for such a war would obliterate the line between defense and aggression as well as the distinction between combatants and noncombatants and between more or less inhuman weapons. Even if such a total war never comes about, its shadow has blurred the lines still further for what is acceptable in "conventional" warfare and for what adversaries can do to one another and to innocent bystanders in times of peace.

In recent years, the blurring of lines between offense and defense has encountered increasing challenge from advocates of so-called nonoffensive or nonprovocative defense.[34] If nations could arrive at balanced and strictly defensive protection against assault, their citizens would no longer have to cope with the economic and psychological burdens of maintaining and being in turn targeted by vast arsenals of offensive weapons; nor would they have to live with the fear that these engender. So far, the movement for nonoffensive defense has focused primarily on measures affecting military preparedness. But the concept of such a form of defense deserves attention in foreign policy more generally—in diplomacy, for instance, as in trade policy and intelligence work. Offensive or provocative policies are precisely those which inspire distrust between adversaries; to the extent that they can be discarded without added danger to national security, everyone stands to gain. There is no necessary link between exercising cautious distrust and acting so as to inspire more distrust among others. On the contrary: adding to the amount of needless distrust makes it harder for all involved to know what dangers genuinely require special attention and impairs the climate needed for resolving conflicts without going to war.

Genuine concern for national security calls, therefore, for extreme caution against giving too free a hand to those who invoke self-defense to legitimate all questionable undertakings. Officials may otherwise assume, without stopping to reflect, that they have no alternative course of action and that the nation's interest calls on them to go against their principles, by planning a disinformation scheme, say, or violating laws they have sworn to uphold.

The Reagan administration's decision in 1985 to send arms to Iran in hopes of assuring the release of U.S. hostages may have begun as just such a well-intentioned effort, however unrealistic, to cut back on the terrorism and violence in the Middle East and to end the suffering for the hostages and their families. But without principled administrative oversight and legislative controls, the doors were opened to practices of bribery, money-laundering, falsification of official documents, and arms-smuggling. As the scandal unfolded, the weakness of the excuses invoking the nation's best interest and the lack of alternatives became apparent; and the role of official secrecy in allowing such excuses to go untested until too late was highlighted once again.

Public officials who are asked for the first time to take part in problematic activities often fall back on yet another standard excuse: that it is not up to them to try to reexamine long-standing national policy. But it *is* up to them, and up to us as well, to take a very close look at all the morally questionable policies that have somehow gained the status of permanence. While some of them may once have been needed as a response to an acute crisis, no one can claim that they are all needed now. Some respond needlessly to ineffective and self-damaging actions by an adversary or are ineffective and thus uncalled for in their own right; others are excessive considering the provocation and thus are especially likely to escalate hostilities; still others are unnecessary because alternative actions will promote national security without hurting innocent bystanders or eroding trust. Together, all such unnecessary tactics damage national security, delay the settlement of regional conflicts, and hinder collective efforts toward se-

curity. They end by forcing government leaders into blatant and embarrassing hypocrisy whenever they claim
self-defense for every form of aggression or deny in public
those acts which they know they sponsor in secret.

Since democracies are expressly committed to justice
and the respect for human rights, they have every reason
to question practices that go against these norms for the
sake of national defense. But whatever their political system, large powers have a special responsibility to avoid
violations that set precedents for others to emulate. A
number of countries have long sought to eschew all such
practices; they, too, have a special function in showing
how to hold the line against them. And all nations, as
suggested in Chapter IV, have a stake in efforts to counteract practices that erode rather than build the confidence
needed for negotiations to further common security. To
the extent that governments fail to do so, concerned organizations and individuals have a critical role to play in
bringing pressure to bear.

As soon as those advancing the strategic argument for
dismissing moral concerns acknowledge that not all shady
practices are necessary for self-defense, and that some may
even damage it, there is already an opening for change.
Strategists have reason, then, to join in reevaluating all
practices linked to defense, if only for the sake of their
own nation's security. In such a process of reevaluation,
more is needed than the customary judgments having
to do with short-range financial and political costs or
with the obstacles to be expected in trying to implement
a policy.

Even before undertaking such judgments, it will be
helpful to begin the process of reevaluation by dividing all
relevant policies into two categories: one containing the
many practices, including those which are purely defensive and confidence-building in nature, that violate no

fundamental moral constraints; and a second category singling out policies that do violate such constraints. About each policy in the second category, one can then ask the three questions set forth in Chapter IV to assist in weighing actions or practices fraught with moral conflict:

1. Is there an alternative policy that might serve the purpose one takes to be justified—in this instance lasting national security—without breaching moral constraints? One, that is, which falls in the first category? Asking this question calls for all involved to look for such alternatives as creatively and imaginatively as possible and to consider what kind of leadership it takes to implement them most effectively.

2. If no alternative policy of nonproblematic nature can be found, what are the arguments by which proponents justify the violations made necessary by the policy under consideration? And what are the counterarguments advanced against it? Where national security is concerned, three subsidiary sets of questions must then be asked:

a. Is the policy one that genuinely serves self-defense? Or is it so ineffective or so likely to backfire as to damage, rather than serve, national security?

b. Is the policy appropriate in light of the provocative policy or action to which it responds? Does it overreact? Does it risk needless escalation? Or is the provocation itself so ineffective or so likely to backfire as to call for a different response or none at all?

c. A consideration of the above questions will eliminate a number of policies as unnecessary or inappropriate. With respect to those remaining ones which still seem necessary in the eyes of proponents, they must be asked to explain on what view of self-defense or national security they base their judgment. And what lines, if any, do they draw with respect to violating fundamental moral constraints on, say, killing noncombatants or cheating on international treaties?

3. As a test of the preceding questions, how would the arguments for and against the answers to each fare if defended in front of an assembly of reasonable critics? Such an assembly would have to be representative of those who bear the costs of the policies at issue—of taxpayers in the nations responsible, for instance, just as much as of potential victims abroad or at home.

Such a process of rethinking and reevaluating existing policies is indispensable to a strategy for peace. It will take time and require the efforts of citizen groups, scholars, and many others in addition to public officials—the more so as line-drawing often calls for considerable fact-finding, analysis, and debate. These efforts of reevaluation, of which mine can be but a small part, offer an alternative path to those who insist either that nothing meaningful can be done, given the genuine threats to survival that so many nations face, or, on the contrary, that nothing *need* be done, since all is well as it is.

There is a better way to reconcile genuine self-defense with the public desire for a principled foreign policy. It is in the power of each nation—and, most urgently, also in the interest of each—to seek ways to reduce excessive, debilitating distrust. And just as many different practices contribute to that distrust, so the collaboration of a great many groups and individuals can bring about a change.

CHAPTER VI

Conclusion

Simone Weil wrote of the Trojan War that "to be out-side a situation as violent as this is to find it inconceivable; to be inside it is to be unable to conceive its end."[1]

Thinking about the threat of nuclear war is like that: when we step outside it in our imagination, we find it inconceivable that a few nations should have come to endanger the entire world in mutual self-defense. And yet, from our own experience of the threat of such violence, we are unable to conceive any end to it other than a catastrophic one, bringing what Kant called the "perpetual peace . . . on the vast graveyard of the human race."

No one can predict whether human beings will achieve enough control over existing and future powers of destruction to avoid the fate of which Kant warned. Momentum is clearly building the world over for doing so. But the chances of success will depend to no small degree on combating two kinds of inertia—one born of despair, the other of complacency. The first is that of the many people who see no hope of overcoming the present crisis. They include liberals as well as conservatives, burned-out peace activists as well as military analysts, those experienced enough to know the difficulties that heighten the threat of war, and young people reluctant even to try thinking about something so ominous and vast. The second form of inertia besets people—at times in high-level positions—convinced that all talk of crisis reflects needless anxiety about a situation that is firmly under control. They place their faith in the nuclear deterrence that has now lasted for over forty years, heedless of warnings by military experts and policy analysts that nations risk a nuclear catastrophe unless they reduce their dependence on deterrence.[2]

In our present crisis, we can afford neither type of inertia. Both are allies of the threat of war, in that they blind people to the many opportunities to work for measures that increase the chance for a lasting peace. For while it may be hard to conceive of a complete end to the threat of nuclear extinction, it is not at all hard to envisage that threat either growing stronger or, on the contrary, being cut back substantially.

It is fully within the capacity of humankind to respond more wisely to the threat of war than by reenacting age-old patterns of entrenched and self-defeating partisanship. We need not accept those patterns passively. We have alternatives to the lowest common denominator as a standard for conduct. There is nothing inevitable about the present levels of distrust and fear, nothing mechanical, nothing irreversible. Such tensions are built up in a thousand ways, by the decisions and failures of many individuals and groups to decide.

Reversing these tensions will require ingenuity and perseverance in pressing for coordinated action on many problems that have long been allowed to drift. To be in a position to do so, nations must now take their bearings from moral constraints that promote collective survival. At least some observance of these constraints has been needed for any family, village, or society to survive, long before one could talk of nation-states, much less of a world community. They must be taken seriously in international relations now that nations risk perishing together.

In stressing the role of moral values, there is no need to join the chorus of nostalgic laments, echoing in our period as they have so often in the past, that moral standards are deteriorating, that young people are not as principled as their elders, that civilization is on the skids. True, there is reason for special concern today about the ability of societies to contend with the combination of problems they now face. But this is not because principled conduct and the ability to cope are somehow withering away; it is, rather, because environmental and military threats to survival are vaster and more urgent than in the past. Previous generations did not take sufficiently strong and principled collective action against these threats while there was still time to keep them in check. Far more is needed today if we are to succeed where they failed. The problems have grown so severe that unless we can marshal a more forceful collective response, all the worst predictions of social collapse may finally come true after all.

Can one expect enough nations and enough people to take such collective action against the threats they now face? Not only to see the threats but to respond vigorously enough? There is room for modest new hope in this respect. It is based on two developments. First of all, nations have a new reason to observe moral constraints in dealing with one another. There were always reasons for doing so and they were always good enough. But the new reason, which was only a hypothesis to Kant when he envisaged that human beings might come to destroy the world, is now utterly real to all. Self-preservation, the most basic human drive, now gives a reason even to those who saw none before to concern themselves with morality. The danger to human existence is no longer an abstraction, something far off in the future or affecting only strangers.

For the sake of our children and our children's children, we now have direct and practical reasons to further what has long been called "the common good," a vision that links philosophies as different as those of Confucius, Aristotle, and Thomas Aquinas, and that echoes in most later philosophies of equal depth and scope.

In the second place, this century has seen the development of strategies, methods, and techniques for bringing about change in such a way as not to injure the fragile level of trust needed for social cooperation toward the common good. We now have models, institutions, and knowledge more fully tested and worked out than in the past. We have learned much more about the causes of conflicts and wars and about ways to prevent them. And recent research has confirmed what experience already showed: that even small groups willing to initiate strategies of cooperation can have an effect far larger than their numbers would initially indicate.[3]

I have spoken of the atmosphere of mixed trust and distrust in which all human interactions take place. Societies thrive neither in an environment of excessive trust nor in one where distrust predominates, any more than living beings survive if the proportion of oxygen in the earth's atmosphere is so low that they cannot breathe or so high that fires rage out of control. Without some mutual trust human beings cannot cooperate for common goals; yet without a measure of skepticism and distrust they are defenseless against exploitation and assault. At either extreme, they lack the capacity to distinguish the cautious distrust needed for making wise choices from conduct that adds needlessly to that distrust in ways that undercut and endanger such choices.

In the past, many societies have gone under or stagnated under such circumstances, while others have recovered or started afresh after a period of retrenchment. Now that nuclear weapons can bring about the end of all life on earth, there may be no further chance to rebuild and try to recover from stagnation or collapse. We are in a situation of dangerously high but often legitimate distrust, not only between East and West but also with respect to the leaders, now and in the future, who may dispose of nuclear weapons, to the accidents that can come about so as to place all at risk, and to the regional conflicts that may escalate so as to precipitate a larger war.

As a result, just as we are going to have to institute imaginative efforts to reverse the damage to our natural environment, so we shall have to be equally imaginative and resourceful in working out ways to defend our nations, resolve conflicts, and achieve social change in ways that do not damage the social environment on which we all depend. Nations have no realistic choice other than that of making an unprecedented effort to break out of what have become outmoded patterns of partisanship.

It is therefore high time that governments, organizations, communities, and individuals take stock and ask to what extent their actions worsen or improve the atmosphere in which cooperation takes place. How can they avoid being free riders damaging a social environment that can tolerate no further injuries? And what can they do to help shift the balance? A broader and deeper perspective, a limited set of fundamental moral constraints, and a practical strategy are indispensable in seeking to improve that climate. Within such a framework, a vast scope for action opens up. It concerns, in every region in the world, military as well as diplomatic, commercial, cultural, and other activities and, for every nation, domestic as well as foreign policy. A comprehensive strategic approach is needed to coordinate action at different levels, in which both citizens and public officials reconsider the role that fundamental moral constraints should play in their nation's domestic and international policies.

Such a comprehensive approach can also help to

broaden the agenda for organizations already dedicated to working for peace. Many of them concentrate so much on some particular conflict or weapons system or reform, or on purely informational or symbolic activities, that they do not see a larger and more practical scope for their work. It is easy, then, to become discouraged, especially after years of effort with little to show in the way of results. Within the context of a strategy for peace, on the other hand, one can choose from among different activities that have practical import, and see the paucity of results in one area as outweighed by advances elsewhere.

Because of the importance of open debate in curtailing shortsighted or biased decisions, censorship and other measures that inhibit debate require opposition as vigorous as that directed toward the violence and deceit that multiply in the absence of free debate. But it is not enough merely to work to cut back on the activities most ripe for change and to debate more marginal ones. We must also take note of, and work to encourage, alternative methods of dealing with conflicts and promoting social change: the growing success of peaceful revolutions, the articulate new forms of resolving conflict that can replace violence in family quarrels as well as in border disputes, the language-teaching and encouragement of travel across every partisan barrier, and the new uses of information technology to promote public debate and to share knowledge.

To be sure, the many individuals caught up in war or forced to live in refugee camps, or suffering from hunger and political oppression, endure daily and direct threats to their personal survival that leave little room for concern about lasting peace or the survival of humanity as a whole. In some nations, those who work for peace and human rights do so at their peril. This places the responsibility even more squarely on those of us who live at peace and in societies protective of free speech. We have special reasons to pursue the debate and to press for the changes that further a strategy for peace. Not only are we freer to do so than others, but we have more to lose, given the risks to the democratic form of government posed by secrecy and by all policies that undermine such a strategy.

There is room for everyone, then, who wants to further such a strategy. And no effort, so long as it respects fundamental moral constraints, is too limited or too personal to contribute in some way to the larger strategy. On the contrary: it is striking how often those who devote themselves to the task of reducing violence and distrust insist, as did Gandhi and King, on the links between personal change and the capacity to bring about social change. Don't start out blindly, they urge; be sure of your own motives and think hard about your methods. If you rush in unprepared, you are likely to fail, defeated or manipulated by forces that you did not understand. If you advocate principles such as that of nonviolence on the public or political level, be sure that you try to observe them in your personal life as well, lest you become entangled in conflict and hypocrisy.

Be prepared, moreover, individuals experienced in these matters advise us, to begin in local and quite piecemeal ways, rather than by backing only the most global changes. You have more power to change yourself than to affect others; likewise, your influence in your community and your nation will be greater than elsewhere. Yes, you want to see the links between what you do and larger contexts. But concentrating from the outset only on the least personal and largest problems imaginable almost guarantees that nothing will get done.

In beginning to work for piecemeal rather than global change as part of a strategy for peace, we can learn from a suggestion of Gandhi's that we carve out spaces or territories in personal relations where violence, say, or deceit will not be used: territories in the family, in the community, with friends and even opponents, where we have more control and also greater responsibility. Such an effort requires that we reconsider the role of violence or deceit in our work—as news reporters or police officers, as public servants or industrial workers, as scientists or executives—and at home, with family and friends, in community service, recreation, and entertainment. If one begins thus, with the personal and the piecemeal, one can then try to expand the reach of these spaces or territories of peace. This is the path already chosen by many individuals, community groups, professional organizations, and religious bodies in searching for ways to establish nonviolence.

I see all those who strive to reduce distrust as working for peace, even if they produce no immediate and direct effect on the nuclear balance of terror. Whether in government offices or at the negotiating table, with children or with adults, in religious or in political groups, in private or public life, the men and women who work to diminish the sway of violence, of deception, of breaches of faith, and of excessive secrecy are all doing the work of peace. They show that the opportunities for such work, should one so choose, are everywhere—and that change can begin, should one so choose, right away.

A POSTSCRIPT

Are we not always too apt to accept too early the dictum that it is already too late to correct a momentous danger to mankind? And is it not of vital importance to be prodded out of such lethargy by a review of the "values we hold most strongly"? Sissela Bok's admirable presentation of the philosophical and political insights that might yet help modern man to face the universal danger of nuclear development offers for fresh scrutiny some grand historical conceptions of universal peace.

But in telling us about these concepts she also seems to appeal to the clinicians and developmentalists among us to contribute what we, so far, have learned both about the necessary strengths and the basic weaknesses that, according to our observations, emerge lawfully in the life cycles of individuals as well as in the generational cycles that hold the individual ones together—life historically, as it were.

Thus we applaud and confirm our speaker's acknowledgment of trust and hope as the first lifelong "virtues" necessary for a potentially sound morality. For here we experience the rare event of finding a developmentalist united in a sentence with Kant: "Compare the way in which trust functions among nations for Kant and in the lives of individuals for Erik Erikson. Both see it as a foundation" (p. 42). But it also becomes clear that such "basic trust," the experience of which we ascribe to the very first stage of life, must still learn to trust itself even as it faces some considerable amount of "sensible mistrust." Together they may well unite at critical moments to provide what Simone Weil is quoted as calling "that halt, that interval of hesitation wherein lies all our consideration for our brothers in humanity," even as Kant calls trust the very reassurance that might permit governments to relinquish what he designates as their "dishonorable stratagems." Kant also acknowledges a basic human need for a "sense of autonomy," the very roots of which we have, in fact, ascribed to the second stage of childhood as the lifelong source of the "virtue" of will.

But in doing so we must also trace the formation early in life of inner frontiers of alienation, for any lasting morality in the individual must also count on a certain severity of conscience. And developing as conscience does through the long human stages of childhood and adolescence, it includes some cruelly moralistic traits, including a deep sense of guilt and thus of lasting mistrust of ourselves as well as of others. This inner human development, we have claimed, contributes to what in social evolution we have come to call pseudospeciation.* This suggests that human groups of various size are apt to project their inner sense of guiltiness and their mutual mistrust on neighboring human collectives—from nations to religions —which then appear to be, in fact, inhuman species of potentially deeply immoral strangers with a persistent readiness for deception, betrayal, and violence. Sooner or later in history it follows that one or the other of these

---

* For a discussion of this concept, see Erik H. Erikson, "Reflections on Ethos and War," and Stephen Jay Gould, "A Biological Comment on Erikson's Notion of Pseudospeciation," both in *Yale Review* 73 (Summer 1984): 481–486; 487–490.

"species" must be destroyed—with whatever available means.

We must now learn to counteract such processes of pseudospeciation, in ourselves as well as in others, by a systematic and mutual study of the lawfulness of individual development (in this connection consider only the study of identity in oneself and in others) and of the history of collective units. We must reinforce this by freely sharing with other nations those universal insights that make sense in all languages (beginning with "I") and can enliven the interrelatedness of all nations in the form of "We."

To indicate here how far Sissela Bok's text supports the study of such thinking, I must refer to a most fitting theme that is used to give a special title to one section of her book: "dirty hands"—a theme then connecting a series of quotations in rather psychoanalytical ways, so to speak. Thus a president of Pakistan says: "You just don't soil your hands unnecessarily unless you can achieve" (p. 184, n. 23), while to a variety of governments is ascribed the view that it may be worthwhile to dirty one's hands in the interest of important goals. Finally (in line with our concept of pseudospeciation) comes the view that "dirty hands calculations seem to come more easily when the victims are foreign" (p. 128).

To appreciate this symbolic meaning of hands it is only necessary to reflect briefly on their developmental evolution and the use of hands in human uprightness, whether in work or in war; or in the most "touching" activities ("shake hands") and the most pious ones ("fold hands") as well as in the most "dirty" and perhaps "sexual" ones. And, indeed, when children are taught the correct use of their hands, they are often shamingly classed with creatures of other species.

In this connection, we have even come to suggest a reformulation of the age-old golden rule. For it must be admitted that such classical formulas as "do as you would be done by" promotes an essentially self-centered point of view. Therefore, we think that we and our colleagues in other countries and cultures must derive from the new insights of developmental studies a golden rule that would permit us (and them) "to do to others what might support their development (at their age or stage, their time or space)" even as it may help us to develop at our age and stage, time and place. Given such a sense of developmental and evolutionary relativity, we believe mankind may sooner or later come to an irreversible sense of a joint nature and, indeed, a mutuality of human fate.

I cannot conclude these brief words without noting that in such a worldwide reorientation we will soon be convinced that of greatest importance for the further evolution of humanity is a more active participation of an enlightened and enlightening womankind in the technical and political planning of the future. It is noteworthy that Sissela Bok could draw on the work of her "political" mother Alva Myrdal, and on her words of encouragement to all who persist in working for peace: "It is not worthy of human beings to give up."

Erik H. Erikson
October 1988

NOTES

INTRODUCTION

1. Erik H. Erikson refers to the "species-wide nuclear crisis" in his address to the American Psychological Association, 1984. See also his "Ethos and War," *Yale Review* 73 (July 1984): 485. For his discussion of the crises of the human life cycle, see his *Childhood and Society* (New York: Norton, 1950); and *Identity and the Life Cycle* (New York: Norton, 1980). Some have argued that the word "crisis" should be used only in a restrictive sense to signify a sudden increase of danger: the heightened fever in a seriously ill patient or an international emergency, as in the Cuban missile crisis. Fen Osler Hampson discusses different definitions of "crisis" seen in such a light, in "The Divided Decision-Makers: American Domestic Politics and the Cuban Crises," *International Security* 9 (Winter 1984–85): 130–165. But to call only emergencies "crises" may lend a false air of reassuring normality to the chronic threat under which we live. I shall therefore hold, with Erikson and many others, that this threat represents a collective crisis. See also my discussion of acute and chronic crises in *Lying: Moral Choice in Public and Private Life* (New York: Pantheon, 1978), pp. 108–122.

2. Michael Howard, "Problems of a Disarmed World," in Herbert Butterfield and Martin Wight, eds., *Diplomatic Investigations* (Cambridge, Mass.: Harvard University Press, 1966), pp. 206–

214. See also his *Weapons and Peace* (London: David Davies Memorial Institute of International Studies, 1983).
3. Bok, *Lying,* p. 26. For views on trust as a public good in economics, see Kenneth J. Arrow, *The Limits of Organization* (New York: Norton, 1974), ch. 4, and Partha Dasgupta, "Trust as a Commodity," in Diego Gambetta, ed., *Trust: Making and Breaking Cooperative Relations* (Oxford: Blackwell, 1988), pp. 49–72.
4. For recent discussions, see Seyom Brown, *The Causes and Prevention of War* (New York: St. Martin's, 1987); Mikhail Gorbachev, *Perestroika* (New York: Harper & Row, 1987); Harvard Nuclear Study Group, *Living with Nuclear Weapons* (New York: Bantam Books, 1983); Russell Hardin et al., eds., *Nuclear Deterrence: Ethics and Strategy* (Chicago: University of Chicago Press, 1985); Michael Howard, *The Causes of Wars* (Cambridge, Mass.: Harvard University Press, 1983); George F. Kennan, *The Nuclear Delusion* (New York: Pantheon, 1985); Anthony Kenny, *The Logic of Deterrence* (Chicago: University of Chicago Press, 1985); Robert S. McNamara, *Blundering into Disaster* (New York: Pantheon, 1986); Independent Commission on Disarmament and Security Issues, *Common Security: A Programme for Disarmament* (London: Pan, 1982); National Council of Catholic Bishops, *The Challenge of Peace: God's Promise and Our Response* (Washington, D.C.: Office of Publishing Services, U.S.C.C., 1983); Jonathan Schell, *The Fate of the Earth* (New York: Knopf, 1982); Gene Sharp, *Making Europe Unconquerable* (Cambridge, Mass.: Ballinger, 1985); Fredric Solomon and Robert Q. Marston, eds., *The Medical Implications of Nuclear War* (Washington, D.C.: National Academy Press, 1986); Raimo Vayrynen, ed., *Policies for Common Security* (Stockholm: Stockholm International Peace Research Institute, 1985).
5. For examples of calls for a new way of thinking, a new ethics, or a transformation of human conscience, see Albert Einstein, letter to Sigmund Freud, 30 July 1932, in *Warum Krieg* (Paris: Institut International de Coopération Intellectuelle, 1933); Jacques Monod, *Chance and Necessity* (New York: Knopf, 1971); Dietrich Fisher et al., *Frieden Gewinnen* (Freiburg: Dreisam-Verlag, 1987); Jean Fourastié, *Essais de morale prospective: Vers une nouvelle morale* (Paris: Editions Gonthier, 1966); Marilyn

French, *Beyond Power: On Women, Men, and Morals* (New York: Summit, 1985); Betty A. Reardon, *Comprehensive Peace Education* (New York: Teachers College Press, 1988); and Richard Smoke with Willis Harman, *Paths to Peace* (Boulder, Colo.: Westview Press, 1987). For a statement calling for several such changes together, see the interview with Jonas Salk by Arianna Stassinopoulos in *Parade Magazine,* Nov. 1984, p. 9: "I now see that the major shift in human evolution is from behaving like an animal struggling to survive to behaving like an animal choosing to evolve. In fact, in order to survive, man *has* to evolve. And to evolve, we need a new kind of thinking and a new kind of behavior, a new ethic and a new morality. It will be that of the evolution of everyone rather than the survival of the fittest." See note 6, Chapter II, for earlier discussions of a moral transformation of humanity that might bring a lasting peace.

6. Norman Cohn relates the course of a number of such mass conversions in *The Pursuit of the Millennium* (New York: Oxford University Press, 1970) and discusses their links to the belief in the imminent end of the world.

7. In *The Imperative of Responsibility: In Search of an Ethics for the Technological Age* (Chicago: University of Chicago Press, 1984) Hans Jonas offers an insightful account of the stretching of values and perspectives called for by the enhancement of human power that technology has made possible.

8. Carl von Clausewitz, *On War,* ed. and tr., Michael Howard and Peter Paret (Princeton, N.J.: Princeton University Press, 1976); Immanuel Kant, "Perpetual Peace: A Philosophical Sketch," in Hans Reiss, ed., *Kant's Political Writings* (Cambridge: Cambridge University Press, 1970).

CHAPTER I. PARTISANSHIP AND PERSPECTIVE

1. In discussing what thoughts this sculpture brings to mind, I have not meant to interpret the artist's own intentions.

2. See Raymond Aron, *Penser la guerre, Clausewitz* (Paris: Gallimard, 1976), 2: 129, 208–210.

3. Aristotle, *The "Art" of Rhetoric,* I, iv, tr. John Henry Freese (Cambridge, Mass.: Harvard University Press, 1975).

4. Thucydides, *The Peloponnesian Wars,* tr. Rex Warner (New

York: Penguin, 1986), p. 244. I have altered the translation slightly to conform more to the Greek. Thucydides describes the change he relates as a "general deterioration of character throughout the Greek world," and as one not merely pitting Spartans against Athenians but as also affecting life within Athens and other city-states, setting fellow citizens against one another.

5. *Ibid.,* p. 245.

6. Stephen Spender, in Richard Crossman, ed., *The God That Failed* (New York: Harper, 1949), pp. 253–254. Compare George Orwell, *Homage to Catalonia* (London: Penguin, 1984).

7. Simone Weil, letter to Georges Bernanos, in Simone Weil, *Selected Essays, 1934–1943,* tr. Richard Rees (London: Oxford University Press, 1962), pp. 171–176.

8. Simone Weil, *The Iliad or the Poem of Force* (Wallingford, Pa.: Pendle Hill, 1956). For discussions of Weil's thought, see Robert Coles, *Simone Weil: A Modern Pilgrimage* (Reading, Mass.: Addison-Wesley, 1987); Simone Pètrement, *Simone Weil, A Life* (New York: Pantheon, 1976); Andreas Teuber, "Simone Weil: Equality as Compassion," *Philosophy and Phenomenological Research* (Dec. 1982): 221–232; George Abbott White, ed., *Simone Weil: Interpretations of a Life* (Amherst: University of Massachusetts Press, 1981).

9. Simone Weil, *Cahiers I* (Paris: Plon, 1951), pp. 153–154.

10. Weil, Letter to Bernanos, p. 174.

11. Weil, *The Iliad,* p. 14.

12. Joseph de Maistre, *Les Soirées de Saint-Pétersbourg* (Paris: J.B. Pélagaud, 1821; 7th ed., 1854), p. 22, my translation. In *On Human Nature* (Cambridge, Mass.: Harvard University Press, 1978), pp. 105–106, Edward O. Wilson concludes, after weighing the evidence regarding human aggression, in a manner that supports the views of Weil and de Maistre, that "aggressive behavior, especially in its more dangerous forms of military action and criminal assault, is learned." But the learning is prepared, in that "we are strongly predisposed to slide into deep, irrational hostility under certain definable conditions. With dangerous ease hostility feeds on itself and ignites runaway reactions that can swiftly progress to alienation and violence."

13. Weil, *The Iliad,* p. 23.
14. Stanley J. Tambiah, *Sri Lanka: Ethnic Fratricide and the Dismantling of Democracy* (Chicago: University of Chicago Press, 1986), p. 120. For differing views on such conflicts, see *Militarization and Indigenous Peoples, Cultural Survival Quarterly* 11, Nos. 3 and 4 (1987). See also Jagat S. Mehta, ed., *Third World Militarization: A Challenge to Third World Diplomacy* (Austin: University of Texas Press, 1985).
15. Henry Kissinger has pointed out persuasively, in *Nuclear Weapons and Foreign Policy* (New York: Harper, 1957), ch. 7, what many have since repeated: that it is not weapons in their own right that cause tensions between nations. Thus England does not fear assault by U.S. nuclear weapons, however numerous they become. England would surely fear such an assault, however, if the United States targeted its weapons on British cities as part of its own military posture.
16. For a discussion of the claims to world domination by Hitler, Stalin, and others, see Hannah Arendt, *The Origins of Totalitarianism* (New York: Meridian, 1958).
17. For a discussion of the dynamics of trust and distrust, see Annette Baier, "Trust and Antitrust," *Ethics* 96 (1986): 231–260; Bernard Barber, *The Logic and Limits of Trust* (New Brunswick, N.J.: Rutgers University Press, 1983); Roger Fisher and Scott Brown, *Getting Together* (Boston: Houghton Mifflin, 1988), ch. 2; Vivien Hart, *Distrust and Democracy: Political Distrust in Britain and America* (Cambridge: Cambridge University Press, 1978); Niklas Luhmann, *Trust and Power* (New York: Wiley, 1980; and Gambetta, ed., *Trust. In The Logic and Limits of Trust,* Barber sets forth three kinds of trust involving different expectations. The most general is "of the persistence and fulfillment of the natural and the moral social orders" (p. 9). Two more specific kinds concern what I have discussed, relating to his distinctions, as expectations regarding rationality and competence on the one hand, and intentions and character on the other. Thomas C. Schelling has argued, in *Choice and Consequence* (Cambridge, Mass.: Harvard University Press, 1984), pp. 210–211, that when it comes to corrupt or criminal organizations, "our concern is to spoil communication, to create distrust and suspicion,

to make agreements unenforceable, to undermine tradition, to reduce solidarity, to discredit leadership, and to sever any moral bond that holds the conspirators together." So long as such measures do not themselves violate moral norms, the reduction in internal trust that they bring about among fellow conspirators will, by interfering with their activities, keep them from eroding trust among members of the larger community.

18. McNamara, *Blundering into Disaster*, p. 6. For a recent treatment of the role of blunders, incompetence, and ignorance in politics, see Richard E. Neustadt and Ernest R. May, *Thinking in Time: The Uses of History for Decision Makers* (New York: Free Press, 1986).

19. Graham Allison, "Second Look: Lessons of the Cuban Missile Crisis," *Boston Globe,* Oct. 26, 1987, p. 13. Allison first studied the Cuban Missile Crisis in *The Essence of Decision* (Boston: Little Brown, 1971). In the *Boston Globe* article, on the occasion of a twenty-five-year reevaluation of the crisis, Allison explains that six—indeed, more—of Robert F. Kennedy's advisers strongly preferred a U.S. strike at the missiles in Cuba, something that would doubtless have killed a number of Russians guarding the missile sites: "In our recent discussions with the Soviets, both Americans and Russians concluded that a Soviet military response would have been inevitable."

20. See Alva Myrdal, "A History of Lost Opportunities," in *The Game of Disarmament* (New York: Pantheon, 1976), ch. III; Richard J. Barnet and Richard A. Falk, eds., *Security in Disarmament* (Princeton, N.J.: Princeton University Press, 1965); Barry M. Blechman and Stephen S. Kaplan, *Force Without War: U.S. Armed Forces as a Political Instrument* (Washington, D.C.: Brookings Institution, 1978); Louis J. Halle, *The Cold War as History* (New York: Harper & Row, 1967); George Kennan, "The American-Soviet Relationship: A Retrospective," in *The Nuclear Delusion,* pp. 102–126; John Lukacs, *A History of the Cold War* (Garden City, N.Y.: Doubleday, 1962); Charles W. Yost, *The Conduct and Misconduct of Foreign Affairs* (New York: Random House, 1972); and books cited in note 4 of the Introduction.

21. See Glenn Seaborg with Benjamin S. Loeb, *Stemming the Tide: Arms Control in the Johnson Years* (Lexington, Mass.: Lexington Books, 1987), pp. 438–472.

22. Jimmy Carter, *Keeping Faith: Memoirs of a President* (New York: Bantam, 1982), pp. 471–473.

23. Thucydides, *The Peloponnesian Wars,* bk. 5, "The Melian Dialogue." The Athenians had previously defeated a similar policy of death and enslavement in the "Mytilenian Debate" (bk. 3).

24. *Ibid.* For a discussion of this passage, see Stanley Hoffmann, *Duties Beyond Borders* (Syracuse, N.Y.: Syracuse University Press, 1981), pp. 11–15; William James, "The Moral Equivalent of War," *Essays in Religion and Morality* (Cambridge, Mass.: Harvard University Press, 1982), p. 163; Michael Walzer, *Just and Unjust Wars* (New York: Basic Books, 1977), pp. 5–13; Simone Weil, "Three Letters on History," in Rees, ed. *Simone Weil: Selected Essays 1934–43.*

25. As late as 1939, when he finished writing his profound and provocative *Twenty Years' Crisis: 1919–1939* (London: MacMillan, 1940), Edward Hallett Carr could still claim that we should not try to base international morality "on an alleged harmony of interests which identifies the interest of the whole community of nations with the interest of each individual member of it" (p. 77). It is much harder to make that claim today. For contemporary challenges to such a view, see, among many others, works as different as "The Challenge of Peace" by the National Council of Catholic Bishops and Richard M. Nixon, *Real Peace* (Boston: Little, Brown, 1984).

26. For recent discussions of alternative approaches to conflict resolution, defense, and social change and for educational programs concerning these approaches, see Brown, *Causes and Prevention of War;* Roger Fisher and William L. Ury, *Getting to Yes* (Boston: Houghton, Mifflin, 1981); Richard W. Fogg, "Dealing With Conflict: A Repertoire of Creative, Peaceful Approaches," *Journal of Conflict Resolution* 29 (1985): 330–358; Howard Raiffa, *The Art and Science of Negotiation* (Cambridge, Mass.: Harvard University Press, 1987); Betty A. Reardon, *Comprehensive Peace Education* and *Educating for Global Responsibility* (New York:

Teachers College Press, 1988); Sharp, *Making Europe Unconquerable;* Smoke and Harman, *Paths to Peace.*
27. Corazon Aquino, Address at Harvard University, Sept. 20, 1986, reported in *Boston Globe,* Sept. 21, 1986, p. 3.
28. William James, "The Teaching of Philosophy in Our Colleges," in *Essays in Philosophy: The Works of William James,* ed. Frederick Burckhardt (Cambridge, Mass.: Harvard University Press, 1978), p. 4. James is speaking of mental perspective in philosophy; I take the shifts, the imagination, and the flexibility that he mentions as applicable to the perception of moral issues.
29. Matthew 7:12. Elsewhere, the Golden Rule is to be found, among other places, in the *Analects* of Confucius, the Hindu classic *Mahabharata,* and the Babylonian Talmud. Immanuel Kant, aware that many would ask why one needs to refer to his moral law when the Golden Rule already prescribes looking at one's actions from the point of view of those affected by them, points out that it cannot give guidance with respect to duties to oneself, or even to the most basic duties to others. See his *Grounding for the Metaphysics of Morals,* in Warner Wick, ed., *Immanuel Kant: Ethical Philosophy* (Indianapolis: Hackett, 1983), p. 37, footnote. John Stuart Mill, on the contrary, aware that many would take his views on ethics to leave out something fundamental, argues that they are in essence no different from the Golden Rule, in *Utilitarianism,* ed. George Sher (Indianapolis: Hackett, 1979), ch. 2. See also Erik H. Erikson, "The Golden Rule in the Light of New Insight," *Insight and Responsibility* (New York: Norton, 1964), pp. 219–243; and Alan Donagan, *The Theory of Morality* (Chicago: University of Chicago Press, 1977), pp. 57–59.
30. Concerning such a role for the imagination, see the words by Percy Bysshe Shelley in *A Defence of Poetry,* in M. F. B. Brett-Smith, ed., *The Four Ages of Poetry* (Oxford: Blackwell, 1947), p. 33. "A man, to be greatly good," he writes, "must imagine intensely and comprehensively; he must put himself in the place of another and of many others; the pains and pleasures of his species must be his own. The great instrument of moral good is the imagination; and poetry administers to the effect by acting upon the cause." Spender, in the passage cited above,

(note 6, Chapter I), likewise stresses the need for "high imaginative understanding" in order to avoid the warping that he had observed in his own thinking and that of so many others. Martha Nussbaum, in *The Fragility of Goodness* (Cambridge: Cambridge University Press, 1986), discusses the need for a lively imagination in seeing a situation "as what it is" and in fully perceiving both sides of a dilemma; she stresses, like Shelley, the indispensable function of poetry in illuminating the role of the imagination for moral reflection. Hannah Arendt discusses the central role of the imagination for Kant in "Imagination," *Lectures on Kant's Political Philosophy*, ed. Ronald Beiner (Chicago: University of Chicago Press, 1982).

CHAPTER II. KANT ON PEACE

1. Kant, "Perpetual Peace," p. 103. In quotations from Kant's works cited below, I have on occasion altered a word or two in the translation to bring it closer to the German meaning. The German text has been reissued along with reviews published between 1796 and 1800 in *Immanuel Kant, Zum ewigen Frieden; mit Texten zur Rezeption, 1796–1800* (Leipzig: Philipp Reclam, 1984). For a discussion of Kant's essay in the light of his philosophy, see John Bourke, "Kant's Doctrine of Perpetual Peace," *Philosophy* 17 (1942): 324–333; Michael W. Doyle, "Kant, Liberal Legacies, and Foreign Affairs," *Philosophy and Public Affairs* 12 (Summer 1983): 205–235, and (Fall 1983): 321–353; Carl Joachim Friedrich, *Inevitable Peace* (Cambridge, Mass.: Harvard University Press, 1948); Otto von der Gablenz, *Kants politische Philosophie und die Weltpolitik unsere Tage* (Berlin: Colloquium Verlag, 1956); Mary Campbell Smith, Introduction to *Perpetual Peace, A Philosophic Essay*, tr. Mary Campbell Smith (London: Sweet & Maxwell, 1903; reissued, New York: Garland, 1972); Wolfgang Schwarz, "Kant's Philosophy of Law and International Peace," *Philosophy and Phenomenological Research* 23 (1962): 71–80; and Howard Williams, *Kant's Political Philosophy* (New York: St. Martin's, 1983), ch. 10.

2. Kant, "Perpetual Peace," p. 96. A central reason why Kant objected so fiercely both to individual suicide and to collective

self-annihilation was that the link to justice and morality would then be lost.

3. *Ibid.*

4. Immanuel Kant, *Grounding for the Metaphysics of Morals,* in James W. Ellington, tr., *Immanuel Kant: Ethical Philosophy* (Indianapolis: Hackett, 1983), p. 30. (This formulation of the categorical imperative was restated by Kant for governments in "Perpetual Peace," p. 122). For a discussion of Kant's view of autonomy, its sources, and its relevance on both a personal, a national, and an international level, see Jerome B. Schneewind, "The Use of Autonomy in Ethical Theory," in Thomas C. Heller et al., *Reconstructing Individualism* (Stanford, Calif.: Stanford University Press, 1986), pp. 64–75. See also Onora Nell, *Acting on Principle* (Berkeley: University of California Press, 1975); and Barbara Herman, "The Practice of Moral Judgment," *Journal of Philosophy* 83 (1985): 414–436. Erik Erikson discusses the development of autonomy in early childhood, in *Identity and the Life Cycle,* as the second major development after that of basic trust. See also his Postscript, p. 154 above.

5. Kant, "Perpetual Peace," p. 108. Kant repeatedly stressed his view of human rights—"Menschenrechte" or "das Recht der Menschen"—as the most sacred institution on earth. See, for example, "Perpetual Peace," p. 101 and "The Contest of Faculties" in Reiss, ed., p. 184.

6. Prominent among works on perpetual peace before Kant were Dante Alighieri, *De Monarchia,* bk. I, tr. Herbert W. Schneider, in Lynchburg College Symposium Readings, vol. 5, *War and Peace* (New York: University Press of America, 1982), pp. 241–261; Erasmus, oration, 1517: *The Complaint of Peace,* tr. Alexander Grieve (London, 1917); King George of Bohemia, *The Universal Peace Organization of King George of Bohemia. A Fifteenth Century Plan for Peace,* (Prague: Czechoslovak Academy of Sciences, 1964); William Penn, *An Essay Toward the Present and Future Peace of Europe* (London: Society of Friends, 1936); Abbé de Saint-Pierre, *Selections from the 2nd Edition of the Abrégé du Projet de Paix Perpetuelle* (London: Sweet & Maxwell, 1927); and Jean-Jacques Rousseau, *A Project of Perpetual Peace,* tr. Edith M. Nuttall (London: Richard Cobden-Sanderson, 1927. For discus-

sions of this tradition, see F. H. Hinsley, *Power and the Pursuit of Peace* (Cambridge: Cambridge University Press, 1963); James Turner Johnson, *The Quest for Peace: Three Moral Traditions in Western Cultural History* (Princeton: Princeton University Press, 1987); R. V. Sampson, *The Discovery of Peace* (New York: Pantheon, 1973).

7. M. Rejai, ed. Mao Tse-tung, *On Revolution and War* (Garden City, N.Y.: Doubleday, 1970), p. 69.

8. For an incisive discussion of these three approaches, see Kenneth Walz, *Man, the State, and War* (New York: Columbia University Press, 1959). Walz (pp. 162–164) takes Kant to focus especially on the second of these levels. I believe that a close reading of Kant's works on war and peace, on ethics, education, and political philosophy will support, rather, the view that he is concerned with the interaction of all three.

9. Summarizing this ancient perception and echoing Kant's language, Arthur Schopenhauer writes, in *On the Basis of Morality,* tr. E. F. J. Payne (Indianapolis: Bobbs-Merrill, 1965), p. 158, that "there are two ways of doing wrong, those of *violence* and of *cunning.* Just as through violence I can kill another, or rob him, or force him to obey me, so by means of cunning I can do all these things, since I confront his intellect with false motives, in consequence of which he must do what he otherwise would not." The quotation from Gandhi is taken from a wall in his ashram in Ahmedabad, now a museum; but he stressed the same thought throughout his writings. See Mohandas Gandhi, *Non-Violent Resistance (Satyagraha)* (New York: Schocken, 1961), p. 88; and Martin Green, ed., *Gandhi in India in His Own Words* (Hanover, N.H.: University Press of New England, 1987), "Two Posers," p. 328.

10. In his writings, John Stuart Mill likewise stresses the primacy of avoiding such forms of harm. He calls moral rules that forbid mankind to hurt one another "more vital to human beings than any maxims, however important, which only point out the best mode of managing some department of human affairs. . . . It is their observance which alone preserves peace among human beings; if obedience to them were not the rule, and disobedience the exception, everyone would see in everyone

else an enemy against whom he must be perpetually guarding himself." See George Sher, ed., *John Stuart Mill: Utilitarianism*, (Indianapolis: Hackett, 1979), p. 58. Friedrich Nietzsche makes a similar claim only to draw a radically different conclusion: in *Beyond Good and Evil*, p. 201, he argues that the perspective from which moral valuations are made is distorted by "the utility of the herd . . . the preservation of the community."

11. In referring to constraints rather than to rules, principles, laws, or prohibitions, I mean to emphasize the variation, from one culture to another, in the degree to which these constraints are formalized and the degree to which exceptions are allowed as, say, in deciding which resorts to violence are allowable in self-defense; and to stress, also, the need in all communities to constrain, hold back, limit the forms of harm to which these constraints refer. Others who speak of moral constraints include Thomas Nagel, who refers to "the general constraints of morality" in *Mortal Questions* (Cambridge: Cambridge University Press, 1979), p. 79; Robert Nozick, who employs the concept of "side constraints" on action, in *Anarchy, State, and Utopia* (New York: Basic Books, 1974), p. 32, to express "the inviolability of others" and prohibit "primarily physical aggressing against them"; and Ruth Anna Putnam, who speaks of a "framework of constraints" in "Weaving Seamless Webs," *Philosophy* 62 (1987): 207–220, at 210.

12. Kant also allowed for capital punishment, though only in retribution for murder, claiming that it was a legitimate exercise of state force. For a critical analysis of this argument by Kant, see Steven S. Schwarzschild, "Kantianism on the Death Penalty (and Related Social Problems)," *Archiv für Rechts- und Sozialphilosophie* 71 (1985): 343–372.

13. Kant, "The Contest of Faculties," in Reiss, ed., p. 187. See also p. 183, where Kant characterizes war as the "source of all evils and moral corruption," and p. 189, where it is described as "the greatest obstacle to morality and the invariable enemy of progress." But Kant had also written of war as promoting human progress by the very distress it brings, forcing individuals and societies to make greater efforts. In his last writings, however, such as "Perpetual Peace" and "The Contest of Fac-

ulties," much of this rhetoric is gone. Hannah Arendt suggests a possible interpretation for Kant's complex view of war, in *Lectures on Kant's Political Philosophy,* ed. Ronald Beiner (Chicago: University of Chicago Press, 1982). According to Arendt, Kant takes war to appear one way to those who take part in the action of war and suffer its consequences, whereas someone assuming the perspective of a spectator can see the design that Providence has for humanity's progress through war and discord. But the double vision recurs, I suggest, even within the perspective of the spectator in Kant's later writings. It is precisely as a spectator taking the largest possible perspective that Kant envisages the end that continued wars could bring to all human undertakings and to "justice itself," in "Perpetual Peace," the *Metaphysics of Morals,* and "the Contest of Faculties."

14. Letter to Maria von Herbert, Spring 1782, in Arnulf Zweig, ed., *Kant: Philosophical Correspondence 1759–99* (Chicago: University of Chicago Press, 1967), p. 189. Kant argued repeatedly that lying constitutes a breach of one's duty not only to oneself and to others but also to humanity and even to duty itself: See the *Lectures on Ethics* recorded by students though never published by Kant himself, tr. Louis Infield (Indianapolis: Hackett, 1963); the *Critique of Practical Reason,* tr. Lewis W. Beck (Indianapolis: Bobbs-Merrill, 1956); and the *Metaphysics of Morals,* in Ellington, ed., *Immanuel Kant: Ethical Philosophy.* For a thoughtful view of morality drawing on Kant's moral philosophy, as well as on Judaism and Christianity, to stress the centrality and universality of moral precepts such as those ruling out harming or killing others and deceit, see Alan Donagan, *The Theory of Morality* (Chicago: University of Chicago Press, 1977).

15. John Stuart Mill, *Utilitarianism,* p. 22. Mill adds: "Yet that even this rule, sacred as it is, admits of possible exceptions is acknowledged by all moralists," the chief of which is to prevent great and unmerited evil. While Mill was wrong in attributing this view to "all moralists," the vast majority do agree with him on the subject of exceptions.

16. Dante Alighieri, *The Divine Comedy, Inferno,* tr. Charles S. Singleton (Princeton, N.J.: Princeton University Press, 1970).

For a chart of the "Slopes of Hell," see Singleton's *Commentary,* 2: 44.

17. Thus in speaking of keeping or breaking promises, Kant often used examples involving a *false* promise to begin with.

18. Immanuel Kant, *Lectures on Ethics,* p. 215. On p. 229 of that work, Kant distinguishes false promises from promises honestly made and then broken: "To cheat is to make a lying promise, while a breach of faith is a true promise which is not kept."

19. Hugo Grotius, *On the Law of War and Peace* (Indianapolis: Bobbs-Merrill, 1925), p. 417.

20. Kant, "Perpetual Peace," p. 100. Kant used the term "Publizität" in referring to the action of making something public. The corresponding term "publicity" can be confusing for contemporary readers, unless they distinguish Kant's usage, and that of John Stuart Mill, John Rawls, and other philosophers, from other senses of the word in political and commercial contexts, as in references to "publicity stunts" and "publicity hounds." For references to different usages of this term and a discussion of its role in ethics, see my books *Lying,* ch. 7, and *Secrets: On the Ethics of Concealment and Revelation* (New York: Pantheon, 1982), ch. 8.

21. Kant drew a distinction between existing laws, even unjust ones, that might require citizens to go to war against their will, and the kind of state that he advocated, in which citizens would be consulted about prospective wars. Thus he explains, in "On the Common Saying: 'This May Be True in Theory, But It Does Not Apply in Practice,' " (Reiss, ed., *Kant's Political Writings*), p. 91, that "each state must be organized internally in such a way that the head of state, for whom the war actually costs nothing (for he wages it at the expense of others, i.e., the people) must no longer have the deciding vote on whether war is to be declared or not, for the people who pay for it must decide. (This, of course, presupposes that the idea of an original contract has already been realized.)"

22. Kant, "Perpetual Peace," p. 126. While Kant holds that actions affecting the rights of others are wrong if they cannot be made public, he adds that the reverse does not follow: actions are not necessarily right if they *can* be made public. Even the

most violent action may be openly performed by individuals or governments so powerful as to have nothing to fear from disclosure.

23. *Ibid.,* p. 96. Compare John Rawls, *A Theory of Justice* (Cambridge, Mass.: Harvard University Press, 1971), p. 379: "The aim of war is a just peace and therefore the means employed must not destroy the possibility of peace or encourage a contempt for human life that puts the safety of ourselves and of mankind in jeopardy. The conduct of war is to be constrained and adjusted to this end."

24. Erikson, *Identity and the Life Cycle,* p. 63.

25. See, for example, Reiss, ed., *Kant's Political Writings,* pp. 53 and 188–189.

26. Niccolò Machiavelli, *The Prince and the Discourses* (New York: Random House, 1950).

27. *Ibid.,* p. 318. For a more absolute claim, see the statement that Machiavelli attributes to the leader of a rebellion in Florence: "If you will observe the way in which men act, you will see that all those who attain great riches and great power have attained them by means of either fraud or force." *The History of Florence,* bk. 3, ch. 12, in Allan Gilbert, tr., *Machiavelli: The Chief Works and Others* (Durham, N.C.: Duke University Press, 1965), p. 1160.

28. Machiavelli, *The Prince,* p. 64. When discussing republics, Machiavelli could nevertheless express caution about the distrust that results from a people's consciousness of having been deceived: "And if it happens that the people have no confidence in anyone, as sometimes will be the case when they have been deceived before by events or men, then it will inevitably lead to the ruin of the state" (*ibid.,* p. 247).

29. *Ibid.,* p. 64.

30. *Ibid.,* pp. 60–61. See also pp. 24, 29–30; and Felix Gilbert, "Machiavelli: The Renaissance of the Art of War," in Peter Paret, ed., *Makers of Modern Strategy from Machiavelli to the Nuclear Age* (Princeton, N.J.: Princeton University Press, 1986).

31. Gandhi gave his *Autobiography* the subtitle *Experiments with Truth* (Boston: Beacon Press, 1977). For the observances he stressed, see his *From Yeravda Mandir: Ashram Observances* (Ah-

medabad: Navajivan, n.d.). Gandhi stressed that truth and truthfulness differ; he thought that he might never attain full knowledge of the former but saw the latter as indispensable in any effort to do so. And nonviolence becomes the more needed as one realizes one may never *be* in the possession of full truth, nor even as close to it as others. To kill or harm others is therefore to risk injuring persons closer to the truth than oneself. For a view of Gandhi's practical strategy, see his *Constructive Programme: Its Meaning and Place* (Ahmedabad: Navajivan, 1941); and R. K. Prabhu and U.R. Rao, eds., *The Mind of Mahatma Gandhi* (Ahmedabad: Navajivan, 1967). See also Joan V. Bondurant, *Conquest of Violence: The Gandhian Philosophy of Conflict* (Berkeley: University of California Press, 1965); Erik H. Erikson, *Gandhi's Truth* (New York: Norton, 1969); Mark Juergensmeyer, *Fighting with Gandhi* (San Francisco: Harper, 1984); and Gene Sharp, *Gandhi as a Political Strategist* (Boston: Porter Sargent, 1979).

32. Adam Michnik, *Letters from Prison and Other Essays* (Berkeley: University of California Press, 1985), p. 78. See also the preface by Jonathan Schell.

33. Kant, "Perpetual Peace," p. 93. Hannah Arendt suggests, in her *Lectures on Kant's Political Philosophy,* that "the ironical tone of *Perpetual Peace* . . . shows clearly that Kant himself did not take his essays on history and politics seriously." Neither Kant's own writings nor their reception by his contemporaries (see note 1 above) supports such an interpretation.

34. Kant, "Perpetual Peace," p. 93.

35. See Kant's discussion of this issue in his essay "On the Common Saying: 'This May Be True in Theory, But It Does Not Apply in Practice,' " in Reiss, ed., *Kant's Political Writings,* pp. 61–92.

36. See note 6 above. It is clear from Kant's *Lectures on Ethics* and his essays that he was familiar with many of these works, especially those by the Abbé St. Pierre and Rousseau.

37. For views on Kant's views on revolution, see Hannah Arendt, *Lectures on Kant's Political Philosophy;* the articles by Lewis W. Beck, Sidney Axinn, John E. Atwell, and C. Dyke in *Symposium: Kant on Revolution, Journal of the History of Ideas* 32

(July–September 1971): 401–440; and Williams, *Kant's Political Philosophy*, ch. 8.
38. Immanuel Kant, "On A Supposed Right to Lie from Benevolent Motives," in *The Critique of Practical Reason and Other Writings in Moral Philosophy*, ed. and tr. Lewis White Beck (Chicago: University of Chicago Press, 1949), pp. 346–350, at 348. In his *Lectures on Ethics*, presented before he had worked out his complete moral philosophy, Kant appears to hold that the case in which someone attempts to force statements from one who seems intent on making improper use of them, in order to misuse them, is the only one in which a lie can be justified. It would be wrong, however, to see the later Kant as being bound to impossible rigidity in responses to practical difficulties. He insisted on an imaginative search for alternative responses that would avert both the need to act immorally and the damage from acting morally. I have discussed this approach in my article "Kant on the Maxim 'Do What Is Right Though the World Should Perish,' " *Argumentation* 2 (February 1988): 7–25.
39. Kant, "Perpetual Peace," p. 124.
40. *Ibid.* For a discussion, see my article cited in note 38 above. Among commentators who have either accepted Kant's claim concerning providence or left it unchallenged are Friedrich, Schwarz, and Smith, cited in note 1 above. Diana T. Meyers argues, in "Kant's Liberal Alliance: A Permanent Peace?" in Kenneth Kipnis and Diana T. Meyers, eds., *Political Realism & International Morality* (Boulder, Colo.: Westview Press, 1987), p. 215, that "Kant's claim that peace is the end of history is highly dubious if it is taken to mean that circumstances will conspire to bring about an enduring peace."
41. See, for instance, the last paragraphs of Kant's *Lectures on Ethics*, clearly intended as a summing up and a peroration, in which Kant speaks of "the ultimate destiny of the human race," which is the Kingdom of God *on earth*. Justice and equity will then rule the world, Kant predicts; but he closes by saying that "the hope of it is still distant; it will be many centuries before it can be attained."
42. See C. W. Friedrich Hegel, *The Philosophy of Right*, tr. T. M. Knox (Oxford: Clarendon Press, 1942), p. 210: "just as

the blowing of the winds preserves the sea from the foulness which would be the result of a prolonged calm, so also corruption in nations would be the product of prolonged, let alone 'perpetual,' peace." See also Joseph de Maistre, *Les Soirées de St. Pétersbourg*, vol. 2; and Benito Mussolini, "Dottrina del Fascismo," in *Enciclopedia italiana* (1932) 14: 847–851: "War alone brings up to their highest tension all human energies and puts the stamp of nobility upon the peoples who have the courage to meet it. . . . War is to the man what maternity is to the woman. I do not believe in perpetual peace; not only do I not believe in it but I find it depressing and a negation of all the fundamental virtues of man."

CHAPTER III. CLAUSEWITZ, WAR, AND STRATEGY

1. Clausewitz, *On War*, p. 75. For commentaries on the views of Clausewitz, see Raymond Aron, *Penser la guerre, Clausewitz* (Paris: Gallimard, 1976); W.B. Gallie, *Philosophers of Peace and War* (Cambridge: Cambridge University Press, 1978); Henry A. Kissinger, *Nuclear Weapons and Foreign Policy* (Boulder, Colo.: Westview Press, 1984), ch. 10; the essays by Peter Paret, Michael Howard, and Bernard Brodie in Clausewitz, *On War;* and H. Rothfels, *Carl von Clausewitz: Politik und Krieg* (Bonn: Duemmler, 1980).
2. Clausewitz, *On War*, p. 192.
3. *Ibid.*
4. *Ibid.*, p. 78.
5. Many have speculated about whether Clausewitz knew Kant's writings and about whether he modeled his dialectical views on Kant or on that of his own contemporary, Hegel. The evidence is far from clear; all that can be said with certainty, since Clausewitz never expressed himself on these subjects directly, is that he had studied with a popularizer of Kant, W. G. Kiesewatter, and that, like all educated Prussians, he was bound to have general knowledge about Kant and about Hegel. See Aron, *Penser la guerre*, pp. 360–371; and Rothfels, *Clausewitz*, ch. 1.
6. Clausewitz, *On War*, pp. 113.

7. *Ibid.*, pp. 120 and 122. See also Peter Paret, "The Genesis of *On War*," *ibid.*, pp 16–18. Clausewitz sees "friction" in terms of a machine metaphor for the conduct of war. Victory comes with speed and smooth functioning *and* with compensating for the friction in one's own campaign, while trying to exploit that besetting one's adversary. Defeat is aided by too much interference by friction that skews one's efforts as it slows them down. He mentions as elements of "friction" aspects of a campaign that can go wrong, such as unexpected turns of the weather or fatigue on the part of troops. He later includes under "general friction" elements of danger, exertion, intelligence, and friction in its own right. He speaks of the "climate of war" (p. 104) and of the "atmosphere of war" (p. 122), in which he once again includes danger and exertion, but adds uncertainty and chance. See Katherine L. Herbig, "Chance and Uncertainty in *On War*," in Michael I. Handel, ed., *Clausewitz and Modern Strategy* (London: Frank Cass, 1986), pp. 95–116, for a discussion of the elements entering into "friction" for Clausewitz.

8. Clausewitz, *On War*, p. 121.

9. Kant, "Perpetual Peace," p. 125: "For all politics must bend the knee before right, although politics may hope in return to arrive, however slowly, at a stage of lasting brilliance."

10. V. I. Lenin, "Socialism and War," *Collected Works* (Moscow: Progress Publishers, 1964), 21: 304. Lenin's views about just or justified wars differ from at least the first and third of three essentials of Christian just war doctrine: that wars, to be just, must be conducted by lawful authorities, be fought for a just cause and animated by a just intention, and not display wrongful or excessive means. For the Christian writings on just war and on perpetual peace, see, respectively, notes 6, Chapter II, and notes 14 and 15 below.

11. V. I. Lenin, *Collected Works*, vol. 24, pp. 163–164. See also pp. 21–26 and vol. 21, pp. 290–294, 316; Mao Tse-tung, *On Revolution and War*, pp. 61–68.

12. Clausewitz, *On War*, p. 579.

13. *Ibid.*, pp. 69, 87, and 610. Just as Kant insisted that politics must bend the knee to right, so Clausewitz insisted that the conduct of war must bend the knee to politics.

14. See Tertullian, *De Idolatria,* tr. J. H. Waszink and J. C. M. van Winden (Leiden: E. J. Brill, 1987), Latin text, p. 62. Jenny Teichman, in *Pacifism and the Just War* (New York: Blackwell, 1987), points out that Christian pacifism differs from the views regarding nonviolence in most religious traditions by holding to a general objection to all war.

15. See Thomas Aquinas, *Summa Theologica,* pt. II-II, q. 40, art. 1. For a discussion of the Christian just war tradition and its contemporary relevance, see James Turner Johnson, *Just War Tradition and the Restraint of War: A Moral and Historical Inquiry* (Princeton, N.J.: Princeton University Press, 1981); Johnson, *The Quest for Peace;* Michael Walzer, *Just and Unjust Wars;* James P. Sterba, "Just War Theory and Nuclear Strategy," in James P. Sterba, ed., *Morality in Practice* (Belmont, Calif.: Wadsworth, 1988); and Teichman, *Pacifism and the Just War.* Reuwen Kimelman discusses biblical sources that distinguish between "mandatory" and "discretionary" wars, in *The Ethics of National Power: Government and War From the Source of Judaism* (New York: National Jewish Center for Learning and Leadership, 1987).

16. In *The Hard Way to Peace: A New Strategy* (New York: Collier, 1961), pp. 200–201, Amitai Etzioni speaks of the danger of nuclear bombs as our common enemy.

17. Clausewitz, *On War,* p. 203. In this regard, Clausewitz speaks against the views of Machiavelli, whom he otherwise admired as the author most worth reading on the conduct of war. David Kahn discusses the role of intelligence for Clausewitz in "Clausewitz and Intelligence," *Journal of Strategic Studies* 9 (1986): 117–126. Compare Machiavelli on intelligence, *The Prince and the Discourses,* pp. 523–526.

18. In *The Gestalt of War* (New York: Dial Press, 1982), Sue Mansfield considers the role of courage for warriors in different cultures. For discussions of courage in relation to other virtues, see Philippa Foot, *Virtues and Vices;* Alasdair MacIntyre, *After Virtue* (Notre Dame, Ind.: Notre Dame University Press, 1981). See Elaine Scarry, *The Body in Pain* (Oxford: Oxford University Press, 1985), pp. 91–108, for a discussion of the role of morale in war, in the context of inflicting and suffering injury.

19. Clausewitz, in *On War,* pp. 169–170, distinguishes four

ways to use examples that are often confused: the example as explanation of an idea; as application of an idea; as support for a statement from cited facts, sufficing to show the *possibility* of something being done or happening; and as detailed presentation for the purposes of proof. Machiavelli, in *The Prince* (p. 55), discusses the role that examples ought to play in the education of a prince.
20. Clausewitz, *On War,* pp. 666–667. For a discussion of Clausewitz on Napoleon, see Jay Luvaas, "Student as Teacher: Clausewitz on Frederick the Great and Napoleon," in Handel, ed., *Clausewitz.*
21. Clausewitz, *On War,* p. 628.
22. Oscar Arias, Nobel speech, *New York Times,* Dec. 11, 1987, p. 2.

CHAPTER IV: TOWARD A STRATEGY FOR PEACE

1. See John Dyson, *Sink the Rainbow!* (London: Gollancz, 1986).
2. Four hundred years before the current debate about the sabotage of the Greenpeace vessel, a French voice spoke out in contempt for another covert undertaking. In "Of the Useful and the Honorable," one of his *Essays,* tr. Donald Frame (Stanford, Calif.: Stanford University Press, 1957), pp. 599–610, Michel de Montaigne tells of some Germans who sent word to the Roman emperor Tiberius offering to rid him of Rome's most powerful enemy, Arminius, by poison. Montaigne quotes the emperor's reply with approval: that the Roman people were accustomed to take vengeance on their enemies by open means, arms in hand, not by fraud and surreptitiously. Montaigne was willing to allow for great variety in human responses and for differences on many matters. But not all things, he claimed, are permissible for an honorable man, even in the service of his nation. He took a firm stand against lying, betrayal of all kinds, violence, and cruelty. "There never was any opinion so disordered as to excuse treachery, disloyalty, tyranny, and cruelty," he insisted, however common these vices may be (p. 176). See my article "Montaigne Today," *Brandeis Review,* 5 (Winter 1986): 17–20.
3. Communities insist on such constraints regardless of whether

members share the principles or have developed the corresponding virtues. If the principle of publicity calls for an associated
virtue, it might be termed "discretion," as I suggest in *Secrets,*
ch. 3, since what is at issue is the capacity to perceive and to
judge what degree of secrecy and openness is called for in different situations. (See note 20, Chapter II, for the meanings of
"publicity.") In my book *Lying,* I refer to four general moral
principles—nonmaleficence, beneficence, fairness, and veracity
—as those to which people appeal most often in seeking to
justify lies. This list overlaps in one respect with the set of
principles discussed here: veracity is part of both lists. The four
general principles are often appealed to, as well, by those who
breach one or more of the moral constraints set forth in the
present book as most fundamental to the survival of human
groups. General principles such as nonmaleficence, beneficence,
and fairness are indispensable as a background to moral deliberation; but they are less tangibly and directly suitable to guiding
international relations than, say, specific contraints on violence
or lying.
4. Micah 6:8; Kant, *Metaphysical Principles of Virtue,* in Reiss,
ed., *Ethical Philosophy,* pp. 112–133. For discussions of Kant's
views about benevolence and helping others, see Barbara Herman, "Mutual Aid and Respect for Persons," *Ethics* 94 (1984):
577–602; and Onora O'Neill, "Kantian Approaches to Some
Famine Problems," in Tom L. Beauchamp and Terry Pinchard,
eds., *Ethics and Public Policy* (Englewood Cliffs, N.J.: Prentice-
Hall, 1983), pp. 205–219.
5. Kant, *ibid.,* p. 116.
6. Confucius, *The Analects,* tr. D.C. Lau (New York: Penguin,
1983), p. 113. See also Tu Wei-Ming, *Confucian Thought* (Al-
bany: State University of New York Press, 1985.) Kant speaks,
in his *Doctrine of Virtue,* of the importance of friendship and
social intercourse in cultivating mutual love and respect; and of
the relationship between one's own social sphere and an all-
encompassing sphere of "cosmopolitan sentiment." (*Ethical
Philosophy,* pp. 135–141). Compare the views of Confucius and Kant with Alexander Pope's last lines in the *Essay
on Man:*

God loves from whole to parts: but human soul
Must rise from individual to the whole.
Self-love but serves the virtuous mind to wake,
As the small pebble stirs the peaceful lake;
The centre moved, a circle strait succeeds,
Another still, and still another spreads;
Friend, parent, neighbour, first it will embrace;
His country next; and next all human race.

7. Kant, *Grounding,* p. 32.
8. See, for instance, John Stuart Mill, *Utilitarianism,* pp. 22, 58, and 59.
9. See, for example, the National Council of Catholic Bishops, "The Challenge of Peace"; Pastoral Letter from the Bishops in the U.S. Methodist Church, 1986; the Evangelical Church in Germany: *EKD Bulletin,* Special Issue, 1981.
10. See John Finnis, Joseph M. Boyle, Jr., and Germain Grisez, *Nuclear Deterrence, Morality and Realism* (Oxford: Clarendon, 1987), p. 382: "The old saying about right and the heavens came from a world-view in which the heavens were not expected ever to fall. As Christians, we believe (and as people acquainted with modern physics, we expect) that they will eventually fall. Yet we also hope that the end of this physical universe, like the death of each human person, will not be the end. As he will raise each person, God will raise up the universe: there will be new heavens and a new earth. . . . In this world, Christians are to prepare for humankind a better life that will not pass away, and every truly realistic moral judgment will be made in that light."
11. Thus, Kant presents what he calls "casuistical questions" of line-drawing in his *Metaphysics and Morals,* concerning marginal cases of, for example, suicide and lying. And in *Nuclear Deterrence,* Finnis, Boyle, Jr., and Grisez discuss the borderline cases that arise in trying to decide who is a combatant and who a noncombatant in war. For a study of the historical and contemporary roles of casuistry, see Albert Jonsen and Stephen Toulmin, *The Abuse of Casuistry: A History of Moral Reasoning* (Berkeley: University of California Press, 1988).
12. *New York Times,* Nov. 10, 1986, p. Al; Nov. 13, p. A21. In

1980 the Shepherds of the Sea reportedly sank a Cypriot whaling ship and two Spanish whalers with mines attached to the hulls, but without inflicting casualties. *Ibid.,* Nov. 10, p. A10.
13. *Lying,* ch. 7; *Secrets,* pp. 112–115.
14. For an analysis of such accountability, see Dennis P. Thompson, *Political Ethics and Public Office* (Cambridge, Mass.: Harvard University Press, 1987), pp. 22–33.
15. Thomas Nagel, "War and Massacre," in *Mortal Questions* (Princeton, N.J.: Princeton University Press, 1979), p. 74. For discussions of moral conflicts, see also Guido Calabresi and Philip Babbitt, *Tragic Choices* (New York: Norton, 1978); Christopher W. Gowans, ed., *Moral Dilemmas* (Oxford: Oxford University Press, 1987); R. M. Hare, *Moral Thinking* (Oxford: Oxford University Press, 1981), chs. 2 and 3; and Nussbaum, *The Fragility of Goodness,* chs. 2 and 3. For reflections on the role of strict moral principles in the face of extreme consequences, see also Rawls, *A Theory of Justice,* p. 303; and Robert Nozick, *Philosophical Explanations* (Cambridge, Mass.: Harvard University Press, 1981), pp. 494–498.
16. For a collection of essays on such measures and an appendix containing excerpts from related treaties, see John Borawski, ed., *Avoiding War in the Nuclear Age: Confidence-Building Measures for Crisis Stability* (Boulder, Colo.: Westview Press, 1986).
17. See the U.S. Joint Chiefs of Staff, *Dictionary of Military and Assorted Terms* (Washington, D.C., 1986), p. 346. For recent works on strategy, see Michael Howard, *The Causes of War;* Kissinger, *Nuclear Weapons and Foreign Policy;* Edward Luttwak, *Strategy* (Cambridge, Mass.: Harvard University Press, 1987); Nixon, *Real Peace;* Peter Paret, ed., with Gordon A. Craig and Felix Gilbert, *Makers of Modern Strategy: From Machiavelli to the Nuclear Age* (Princeton, N.J.: Princeton University Press, 1986); Thomas C. Schelling, *The Strategy of Conflict* (Cambridge, Mass.: Harvard University Press, 1960)); Robert S. Wood, "The Conceptual Framework for Strategic Development at the Naval War College," *Naval War College Review* 40 (Spring 1987): 4–16.
18. For discussions of such policies, see Barry M. Blechman and Stephen S. Kaplan, *Force Without War: U.S. Armed Forces as a Political Instrument* (Washington, D.C.: Brookings Institution,

1978); and Yuan-li Wu, *Economic Warfare* (New York: Prentice-Hall, 1952).

19. In "The Limits of Confidence," in Borawski, ed., *Avoiding War*, pp. 184–198, Jim E. Hinds describes how distrust can increase rather than decrease when agreements designed to serve as confidence-building measures become, rather, sources of confrontation and frustration. See Anthony Pagden, "The Destruction of Trust and Its Economic Consequences in the Case of Eighteenth-Century Naples," and Diego Gambetta, "Mafia, the Price of Distrust," in Gambetta, ed., *Trust* (pp. 127–141 and 158–175), for studies of strategies of destroying rather than building trust. Niklas Luhmann has pointed, in "Familiarity, Confidence, Trust: Problems and Alternatives," in the same volume, pp. 94–107, to a possible distinction between the concepts of "confidence" and of "trust": "Both concepts refer to expectations which may lapse into disappointments. . . . If you do not consider alternatives (every morning you leave the house without a weapon!) you are in a situation of confidence. If you choose one action in preference to others in spite of the possibility of being disappointed by the action of others, you define the situation as one of trust." Most references to "confidence-building measures" as to trust among nations use the two concepts interchangeably, however.

20. I have discussed confidence-destroying measures in "Distrust, Secrecy, and the Arms Race," *Ethics* 95 (April 1985): 712–725.

21. Kant, "Perpetual Peace," pp. 107–108.

22. For discussions of collective action and the problem of free riders, see Robert Goodin, *The Politics of Rational Man* (New York: Wiley, 1976); Mancur Olson, *The Logic of Collective Action* (Cambridge, Mass.: Harvard University Press, 1965). For the complexity that secrecy adds, see my *Secrets*, ch. 8.

CHAPTER V: OBJECTIONS FROM A PRACTICAL POINT OF VIEW

1. Sigmund Freud, "Reflections upon War and Death," from *Character and Culture*, ed. Philip Rieff (New York: Collier, 1963), p. 112.

2. *Ibid.*, p. 33.

3. Quoted in Carr, *Twenty Years' Crisis*, p. 97.

4. See Raymond Aron, *Peace and War: A Theory of International Relations* (Garden City, N.Y.: Doubleday, 1966); George Kennan, *American Diplomacy, 1900–1950* (Chicago: University of Chicago Press, 1984); Hans J. Morgenthau and Kenneth Thompson, *Politics Among Nations* (New York: Knopf, 1985); and Reinhold Niebuhr, *Moral Man and Immoral Society* (New York: Scribner, 1960)

5. George Kennan, "Morality and Foreign Policy," *Foreign Affairs* (Winter 1985/86): 205–218, at p. 207. For a discussion of the role of morality in policy, see Aron, *Peace and War;* Charles R. Beitz, *Political Theory and International Relations* (Princeton, N.J.: Princeton University Press, 1979); Marshall Cohen, "Moral Skepticism and International Relations," in Charles Beitz et al., eds., *International Ethics* (Princeton, N.J.: Princeton University Press, 1985); J. E. Hare and Carey B. Joynt, *Ethics and International Affairs* (New York: St. Martin's, 1982); Hoffman, *Duties Beyond Borders;* Nye, *Nuclear Ethics;* Walzer, *Just and Unjust Wars.*

6. Kennan, *American Diplomacy*, pp. 89–101.

7. Woodrow Wilson, Address, May 11, 1914 in memory of those who lost their lives at Vera Cruz, in Ray S. Baker and William E. Dodd, *The New Democracy: Presidential Messages, Addresses, and Other Papers (1913–1917) by Woodrow Wilson* (New York: Harper, 1926), 1: 104. John M. Blum points out, in *Woodrow Wilson and the Politics of Morality* (Boston: Little, Brown, 1956), p. 84, that Wilson had given little thought to foreign policy during his years of preparing for public office.

8. Aristotle, *Nicomachean Ethics,* tr. Terence Irwin (Indianapolis: Hackett, 1985), 1109a, p. 51.

9. Jeremy Bentham, *Introduction to the Principles of Morals and Legislation,* ed. J. H. Burns and H. L. A. Hart (London: Athlone, 1970), p. 156, footnote.

10. La Rochefoucauld, *Maximes et réflexions diverses* (Paris: Gallimard, 1972), p. 79. For a discussion of hypocrisy and of Molière's portrayal of hypocrites, see Judith N. Shklar, *Ordinary Vices* (Cambridge, Mass.: Harvard University Press, 1984), ch. 2.

11. La Rochefoucauld, *Maximes,* p. 103. For a view of the life-preserving nature of a capacity for humor even in extreme circumstances, see Viktor Frankl's account of his recourse to it to stave off despair while at Auschwitz, in *Man's Search for Meaning* (New York: Washington Square Press, 1985), pp. 63–64.

12. Barry Feinberg, ed., *The Collected Stories of Bertrand Russell* (New York: Simon & Schuster, 1972), p. 332.

13. See E. H. Gombrich, *Myth and Reality in German War-Time Broadcasts* (London: Athlone, 1970), p. 19.

14. See, for example, Hans Morgenthau's rules of diplomacy that would, if adopted, help nations stave off war. The third rule asks leaders to try to adopt the point of view of other nations.

15. Harold Nicolson, *Peacemaking, 1919* (London: Constable, 1933), chs. 3 and 4.

16. *Ibid.,* pp. 36–37.

17. Michael Walzer takes this position in "Political Action: The Problem of Dirty Hands," *Philosophy and Public Affairs,* 2 (1973): 160–180. For discussions of issues of dirty hands, see Alan Donagan, *The Theory of Morality* (Chicago: University of Chicago Press, 1977), pp. 180–189; Alan Goldman, *The Moral Foundations of Professional Ethics* (Totowa, N.J.: Rowman and Littlefield, 1980), pp. 62–76; Stuart Hampshire, "Public and Private Morality," in *Public and Private Morality,* Stuart Hampshire et al., eds. (Cambridge: Cambridge University Press, 1978), pp. 23–54; Terence C. McConnell, "Moral Blackmail," *Ethics* 91 (1981): 544–567; Thomas Nagel, "Ruthlessness in Public Life," in Hampshire, et al., eds., *Public and Private Morality,* pp. 75–92; Thompson, "Democratic Dirty Hands," in *Political Ethics,* pp. 11–39; Bernard Williams, "Politics and Moral Character," in *Moral Luck* (Cambridge: Cambridge University Press, 1981).

18. Walzer, "Dirty Hands," pp. 166–168.

19. Max Weber, "Politics as a Vocation," in H. H. Gerth and C. Wright Mills, tr. and ed., *From Max Weber: Essays in Sociology* (New York: Oxford University Press, 1948), pp. 77–127. In this article, Weber warns against what would come of efforts to establish war guilt: "A nation forgives if its interests have been damaged, but no nation forgives if its honor has been offended, especially by a bigoted self-righteousness" (p. 118).

For discussions of Weber's essay, see Hoffman, *Duties Beyond Borders,* ch. 1; Walzer, "Dirty Hands," pp. 176–178; and Gene Sharp, *Gandhi as a Political Strategist,* ch. 11.

20. Weber, p. 122. Weber's young friend Georg Lukacs had just undergone such a shift during the war years. In late 1918, joining the Communist party in Hungary, Lukacs publicly espoused what he had earlier explicitly rejected: the use of terror as a legitimate means of achieving a classless society and, thereby, ultimately peace. See his *Tactics and Ethics: Political Essays 1919–1929* (New York: Harper & Row, 1972).

21. Weber, p. 126.

22. A murky hint near the end of Weber's essay is especially likely to confuse readers: he now indicates that the most admirable politicians somehow unite the two ethics that he had earlier called irreconcilable. Without indicating how this feat is to be accomplished, Weber simply states that the ethic of ultimate ends and the ethic of responsibility are then "not absolute contrasts but rather supplements, which only in unison constitute a genuine man—a man who *can* have the calling for politics" (p. 127). Stanley Hoffman argues persuasively in *Duties Beyond Borders,* in response to Weber, that his view that the ethics of political action inevitably entails the use of evil means, is both an abdication of moral judgment and a confusion of moral judgment.

23. See, for example, the remark attributed to General Mohammad Zia-al-Haq, former president of Pakistan, when asked whether his government was developing a nuclear capacity and training Sikh terrorists to operate in India. No, he said, "you just don't soil your hands unnecessarily unless you can achieve." *New York Times,* October 21, 1985, p. A8.

24. The concept of "dirty hands" in discussions of the ethics of public and professional life is not the same as or limited to what is meant in the law of equity by "unclean hands." In the case of *Carmen* v. *Fox Film Corporation,* for example, Circuit Judge Rogers held that "The maxim that one who comes into equity must come with clean hands—means that equity will refuse its aid in any manner to one seeking its active interposition if he has been guilty either of unlawful or inequitable conduct re-

specting the subject matter of the litigation." See Richard H. Field, Benjamin Kaplan, and Kevin M. Clermont, *Materials for a Basic Course in Civil Procedure* (Mineola, N.Y.: Foundation Press, 1984), p. 371.

25. For an example of reasoning from extreme cases to general practices in social research in order to justify dirty-hands policies, see Carl B. Klockars, "Dirty Hands and Deviant Subjects," in Carl B. Klockars and Finbarr W. O'Connor, eds., *Deviance and Decency: The Ethics of Research with Human Subjects* (Beverly Hills, Calif.: Sage, 1979), pp. 261–282.

26. As indicated in Chapter II and in note 10, Chapter II, and note 8, Chapter IV, Kant and Mill agree about the costs of acts that help to poison the atmosphere, and take for granted that they often contribute to a cumulative process of deterioration. Many modern commentators argue as if choices concerning such acts are made in a social near-vacuum and concern, at most, the agents themselves and those on whom their acts might have immediate impact.

27. In *The Evolution of Cooperation* (New York: Basic Books, 1984), Robert Axelrod sets forth a penetrating analysis of how cooperative strategies repaying noncooperation "tit for tat" might work and even "invade" strategies in which cheating and defection are the rule. At one point (p. 137), however, he speaks as if the response to cheating or noncooperation must be "an eye for an eye." He offers no argument for this assertion, and much of what he says in the rest of the book indicates that he often has in mind some form of reciprocal noncooperation that need not be a response in kind. I would wish to underline the notion of reciprocity, while submitting that responding in kind, when the original form of noncooperation represents a violation of a fundamental moral constraint, would be not only wrong (with the limited exceptions indicated in this and earlier chapters) but distinctly counterproductive from the point of view of establishing a reciprocal process of cooperative interactions.

28. Jonathan C. Randal, *Going All the Way: Christian Warlords, Israeli Adventurers, and the War in Lebanon* (New York: Vintage, 1983), p. xi.

29. Machiavelli, *Discourses*, p. 528.

30. Quoted by Edward F. Sayle in "The Historical Underpinnings of the U.S. Intelligence Community," *International Journal of Intelligence and Counterintelligence* 1 (1986): 1–27 at p. 2.

31. See Erasmus, *The Complaint of Peace*. After castigating clergy and scholars on different sides of the religious wars then raging in Europe for justifying them by twisted references to scripture and ancient authors, Erasmus insists that only purely defensive wars qualify as "just and necessary" in the strict sense of those words (p. 58). Kant was equally scathing about the latitude with which Grotius, Pufendorf, Vattel, and others were quoted in order to justify military aggression, and saw self-defense as the one exception to his rejection of the use of military forces. "Perpetual Peace," pp. 95 and 103.

32. Thus the pastoral letter of the U.S. Catholic bishops, *The Challenge of Peace,* states: "As both Pope Pius XII and Pope John XXIII made clear, if a war of retribution was ever justifiable, the risks of modern war negate such a claim today" (p. 707). See also J. E. Hare and Carey B. Joynt, *Ethics and International Affairs* (New York: St. Martin's, 1982), ch. 3.

33. For a discussion of this distinction, see Onora O'Neill, "Lifeboat Earth," in Charles R. Beitz et al., eds., *International Ethics* (Princeton, N.J.: Princeton University Press, 1985), pp. 262–281; and Teichman, *Pacifism and the Just War,* ch. 8. Teichman views acts of self-defense as those acts of self-preservation against an immediate threat from an agent who intends to kill or seriously injure you, and that themselves consist of immediate counterattacks directed at the agents and at no one else. David Wasserman, in "Justifying Self-Defense," *Philosophy and Public Affairs,* Fall 1987, pp. 356–378, analyzes the legal and moral support for allowing certain forms of killing in self-defense. Michael Walzer, in *Just and Unjust Wars,* ch. 16, distinguishes a category of "supreme emergencies" in which peoples or nations confront imminent and serious danger.

34. See Randall Forsberg, "Non-Provocative Defense: A New Approach to Arms Control" (Brookline, Mass.: Institute for Defense and Disarmament Studies, 1987); Kenny, *The Logic of Deterrence,* ch. 9; Sharp, *Making Europe Unconquerable;* and the bibliographies and articles in *NOD, Non-Offensive Defense,* an

international newsletter published by the Copenhagen University Center of Peace and Conflict Research; Stephen J. Flanagan, "Non-Provocative and Civilian-Based Defenses," in Joseph S. Nye, Jr., et al., *Fateful Visions* (Cambridge, Mass.: Ballinger, 1988), ch. 5.

CHAPTER VI: CONCLUSION

1. Simone Weil, *The Iliad*, p. 22.

2. For an exploration of the chances of a catastrophic nuclear war coming about, and of different approaches to reducing these chances., see Nye et al., eds., *Fateful Visions*.

3. In *The Evolution of Cooperation*, Robert Axelrod concludes (p. 173), that "cooperation can get started even by a small cluster of individuals who are prepared to reciprocate cooperation, even in a world where no one else will cooperate." Once this happens, he adds, such cooperation can "protect itself from invasion by uncooperative strategies." Axelrod ends by stressing that the process of trial and error in learning to cooperate is slow and painful—so much so that our societies may not have time to wait for blind evolutionary processes to work themselves out, unless human beings use their foresight to speed up the process of evolution in this respect (p. 191).

SUBJECT INDEX

INDEX OF NAMES

Smoke, Richard, 159n, 164n
Solomon, Fredric, 158n
Spender, Stephen, 8–9, 160n, 164–65n
Stassinopoulos, Arianna, 159n
Stead, W. T., 113
Sterba, James P., 176n

Tambiah, Stanley J., 12, 161n
Teichman, Jenny, 176n, 186n
Tertullian, 64n, 176n
Teuber, Andreas, 160n
Thompson, Dennis P., 180n, 183n
Thompson, Kenneth, 182n
Thucydides, 7, 8, 20, 21, 159–160n, 163n
Tiberius, 177n
Tolstoy, Leo, 22, 34
Toulmin, Stephen, 179n
Tu Wei-ming, 178n

Ury, William L., 163n

Vattel, Emmerich, 186n
Vayrynen, Raimo, 158n
Voltaire, xiv

Walz, Kenneth, 167n
Walzer, Michael, 126, 163n, 176n, 182n, 183n, 184n, 186n
Wasserman, David, 186n
Watson, Paul, 90–91
Weber, Max, 126–27, 183–84n
Weil, Simone, 9–12, 145, 154, 160n, 161n, 163n, 187n
White, George Abbott, 160n
Wick, Warner, 164n
Wight, Martin, 157n
Williams, Bernard, 183n
Williams, Howard, 165n, 173n
Wilson, Edward O., 160n
Wilson, Woodrow, 112–14, 117–18, 120, 123–24, 182n
Wood, Robert S., 180n
Wu, Yuan-li, 181n

Yost, Charles W., 162n

Zia-al-Haq, Gen. Mohammad, 184n
Zweig, Arnulf, 169n

ABOUT THE AUTHOR

Sissela Bok was born in Sweden and educated in Switzerland, France, and the United States. She received a Ph.D. in philosophy from Harvard University. She has taught courses in ethics and decision making at Harvard Medical School and the John F. Kennedy School of Government, and has been associate professor of philosophy at Brandeis University since 1985. She is the author of *Lying: Moral Choice in Public and Private Life* and *Secrets: On the Ethics of Concealment and Revelation.* Her biography of her mother, Alva Myrdal, published in Sweden in 1987, will be published in the United States in 1990.